de to

ern

ing

A Practical Guide to
Modern Gamekeeping

Essential information for part-time
and professional gamekeepers

J C Jeremy Hobson
With a Foreword by Alan Titchmarsh

howtobooks

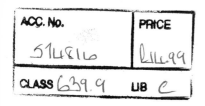
Published by How To Books Ltd.
Spring Hill House, Spring Hill Road
Begbroke, Oxford OX5 1RX
United Kingdom
Tel: (01865) 375794
Fax: (01865) 379162
info@howtobooks.co.uk
www.howtobooks.co.uk

First published 2012

British Library Cataloguing in Publication Data
A catalogue record of this book is available from the British Library.

ISBN: 978 1 84528 497 8

Produced for How To Books by Deer Park Productions, Tavistock, Devon
Designed and typeset by Mousemat Design Ltd
Photos by author unless otherwise credited
Printed and bound by Graficas Cems, Villatuerta (Spain)

NOTE: The material contained in this book is set out in good faith for general guidance and no liability can be accepted for loss or expense incurred as a result of relying in particular circumstances on statements made in the book. Laws and regulations are complex and liable to change, and readers should check the current position with relevant authorities before making personal arrangements.

Contents

Acknowledgements

Despite being involved with shoot management in one form or another for well over 30 years, it is impossible to keep up-to-date with every single one of the changes and trends appertaining to modern gamekeeping and so I have cause to be grateful to many people with regard to the compilation of this book.

Firstly, I would like to thank Alan Titchmarsh who, in his role as a patron of the National Gamekeepers' Organisation (NGO), has very graciously provided the Foreword for this book – his astute observations succinctly encapsulate the role of the modern-day gamekeeper. Thanks too to Tim Weston and the committee of the National Gamekeepers' Organisation for answering my questions, providing valuable contacts and giving me permission to quote from their website; also, Charles Nodder, head of press and public relations, for his erudite information on the aims and objectives of the NGO – in fact, all connected with that particular organisation have been incredibly supportive of this project and I am extremely grateful.

I am grateful to James Horne, Managing Director of GunsOnPegs and David Steel, partner and Head of Sporting at Smiths Gore for their invaluable assistance and permission to quote from the Shoot Benchmarking Survey; Jeffrey Olstead, Head of Publications at the British Association for Shooting & Conservation (BASC) for permission to mention and refer to their various Codes of Practice; Glynn Evans, Head of Gamekeeping at BASC, for spending a great deal of his time in bringing me up-to-date with the latest information. Another person who has been extremely generous with his time and knowledge – and also in allowing me the use of photos – is Dr Mike Swan, Head of Education at the Game & Wildlife Conservation Trust (GWCT).

Some sections, notably the information found in the chapters dealing with game crops and diseases, are an amalgam of my own knowledge and casual conversations had between keepers, farmers and veterinary surgeons over recent months. Their un-named input is much appreciated.

On the veterinary front, I should particularly like to thank Victoria Roberts BVSc MRCVS for her kindness in reading through my first draft of Chapter 9, altering what was erroneous, making constructive comments and providing some extremely valuable photographic illustrations. I must, in addition, also thank Mark

Elliott BVSc VetMFHom MRCVS for all his help and advice. Mark is a co-founder of the Gamebird Veterinary Group (www.gamebirdvetgroup.co.uk), a rapidly expanding collaboration of practices linking together vets with a particular interest in gamebird health.

No matter how relevant any written information might be, words are always enhanced by photographs of the right calibre. In obtaining these, I have been fortunate indeed in being able to prevail upon the expertise of Alan Waugh, Philip Watts and Elliot Hobson. Patrick Pinker Game Farms Ltd, Iron Acton, Bristol, supplied the photographs of the fox cage trap and the galvanised hopper while Richard Barnes, Manager at Kings Game Cover and Conservation Crops (a division of Frontier Agriculture, Norfolk), was extremely generous in providing several of the photos used to illustrate text material in Chapter 10. Stuart and Lorraine Fairhead of Heath Hatcheries, Mildenhall, Bury St Edmunds, Suffolk were kind enough to respond very promptly to my request to use some photos from their website (www.heathhatcheries.co.uk). The photos themselves, however, were actually taken by Alan Waugh and so I thank all three involved for granting permission to use them in Chapter 6. In Chapter 12, 'The Gamekeeper's Dog', there are some photographs generously supplied by Sue Knight, a fellow contributor to *The Countryman's Weekly*, and also one of the show ring at Crufts taken by Mark Ridley of TSI Photography – they illustrate the text wonderfully; as does that from Reedlands Retrievers taken on location at the *Downton Abbey* film set. Thanks too to David S. D. Jones for the archive photos in the introduction.

Photographs cannot, of course, be taken if there is no subject matter! For that I am eternally grateful to Charlie Adam at Raker Ltd, West Sussex; Robjent's, Stockbridge, Hampshire; Stuart Fairhead; Kevin Hubbard; Mark Philips; Mark Munday and Mike Davies.

Finally, whilst every effort has been made to ensure that permission has been sought and acknowledgements given from no matter what source, should anyone reading this book feel that is not the case, I can only offer my apologies and the promise that, if they will be kind enough to get in touch with me via the publisher, I will most certainly make amends in future reprints.

Author's Note

It is important to note that, wherever possible, I have tried to avoid using inclusive pronouns (e.g. 'his or her' and 'he and she') in the text: sometimes though, for pure convenience, I have used 'he' as a neutral pronoun and absolutely no sexist inference should be taken from this.

Also, unless specifically stated, the reference to any company, organisation, product or publication in this book does not constitute an endorsement or recommendation.

J. C. Jeremy Hobson
Summer 2012

The National Gamekeepers' Organisation

The National Gamekeepers' Organisation (NGO) was founded in 1997 by a group of UK gamekeepers who felt that their profession was threatened by public misunderstanding and poor representation. From that time on it has been 'run by gamekeepers for gamekeepers' and it now has 6,000 gamekeeper members and a further 10,000 supporters. The NGO's main aim is: 'To promote, improve and protect gamekeeping in the United Kingdom, thereby securing a thriving long-term future for the profession.'

It does this by providing proper national representation of the gamekeeping profession. The NGO has become the first point of contact for outsiders seeking to approach the gamekeeping world for information or advice and it is now regularly consulted by the government and other authorities on issues concerning wildlife management. The NGO retains professional lobbyists and PR advisors but prides itself on fielding working gamekeepers to attend meetings and to speak for the profession whenever possible.

Assisting gamekeepers to do their jobs is also a key NGO objective and members receive regular informative magazines and attend regional and national meetings where issues of importance to gamekeepers are discussed. An associated company, NGO Training Limited, runs good value courses on subjects like predator control, game meat hygiene, deer management and gun safety. In recent years the organisation has also offered free training to the police to improve their understanding of gamekeeping.

Legal advice and assistance with applications for firearms certification is provided to members and a third party insurance for leisure shooting activities is included in the modest annual subscription. The NGO has also helped to set up a jobs' register for gamekeepers, which is now run by the Gamekeepers' Welfare Trust. Another associated charity, the NGO Educational Trust, is involved in teaching thousands of schoolchildren about gamekeeping each year by providing materials for the National Curriculum and organising dozens of estate visits to meet gamekeepers and to hear about their work.

Whilst the NGO actively works to counter any adverse publicity, it also recognises that the profession can be let down by foolish or improper behaviour. It upholds the Code of Good Shooting Practice and members who break the law are likely to find their membership terminated. The NGO believes that the good name of gamekeeping is paramount. Because, thanks to the NGO, gamekeeping is now so much better represented, informed and defended, the profession is stronger than ever before and in turn provides a good basis for the defence of shooting and the continuation of a much valued way of life. All this activity is well summed up in the organisation's by-line: 'Keeping the Balance'.

For more information and membership enquiries, contact:

The National Gamekeepers' Organisation, PO Box 246, Darlington, DL19FZ.

01833 660869

www.nationalgamekeepers.org.uk

Foreword

Alan Titchmarsh MBE, VMH, DL

Growing up in Yorkshire, the grouse moors were my playground, and as we ran through the heather as children with our game little dog at our heels we'd frequently put up a brace of grouse and hear the 'go-back, go-back!' cry that stopped us in our tracks.

Not everyone is close to moorland, but there are few people who have not taken a walk in the woods and marvelled at the beauty of this particular brand of countryside: sheets of bluebells, a canopy of lime-green foliage that filters the light, the startled 'pook' of a pheasant as it is disturbed and takes flight – all wonderfully natural. The trouble is that nature often needs a helping hand and, as any gamekeeper knows, there is hardly an inch of the British Isles that is not managed to keep it looking 'natural'.

Woodland and farmland, moorland and fen are all looked after by twenty-first-century countrymen and women who understand concepts like 'stewardship' and 'husbandry' and who also understand the importance of their custodianship.

There are those who look upon shooting and fishing as barbaric sports, but look further and you will discover that coverts and woodlands are planted and thinned, farm headlands are left wild to help butterflies and insects as well as game, and the weed in rivers is cut to encourage the invertebrate life that supports fish. Gamekeeping is about far more than sport; in its broadest sense it is, at its core, thoughtful and responsible countryside management, and without the keepers doing their bit it would not be long before all forms of native wildlife suffered.

The motto of the National Gamekeepers' Organisation, of which I'm proud to be a patron, is 'keeping the balance' and I know of no gamekeepers who are not countrymen to their fingertips. They observe, they consider, they cherish and they do more than most to look after out woodlands and hedgerows, our moorlands and fens.

Theirs is not an easy job – out in all weathers and misunderstood by many townies who are further removed from the countryside and its workings than they have ever been, thanks to increasing use of technology which keeps them housebound. They need never go out if they so choose – remaining glued to the screen of a mobile phone, a computer or a television.

But those who do realise that human intervention need not always be irresponsible and thoughtless can see just what benefits can accrue from the wise management of our natural resources, and Jeremy Hobson does much in this book to apprise us all of the modern approach to keepering, from raising birds and habitat management to choosing coats and boots and training dogs. It is all here, and a fascinating read it is – both for those in the know and those who are curious to learn all about it.

As Alexander Pope so wisely said: 'In all, let nature never be forgot.'

Introduction

It might seem strange to begin a book on modern gamekeeping methods with a description of how things used to be a century or more ago, but, to fully understand the situation in the present day, you first need to understand the past and so I make no apologies for including a little bit of, what I hope, is interesting history!

How Gamekeeping Evolved

Early shooting with muzzle-loading guns consisted of partridges being walked-up and shot over fields of roots and stubble by wealthy landowners assisted by their pointer and setter dogs.

The partridge was the most abundant quarry at the time due to farming practices instigated in the 1700s by the likes of Lord ('Turnip') Townsend which created an ideal habitat in which birds could feed and breed. By the mid-1800s they were still the main game birds to be seen in the countryside and were protected by a 'close' season which ran from 31 January to 31 August (much as they are today).

Lock, stock and smoking barrels!

Developments in the gun-making world had, by this time, led to the invention of the breech-loading shotgun – a sporting gun that broke in two and allowed the insertion of ready prepared cartridges, each containing their own ignition, charge and shot load. The gun had many advantages; not least in its ability to be loaded and fired more quickly. This in turn, eventually resulted in the sport of partridge shooting changing from that of 'walked-up' to 'driven' – a practice preferred by many sportsmen who were looking for more difficult and challenging fly game which was, in their opinion, best achieved by having birds appear as crossing or approaching shots rather than, as had previously been the norm, going away.

The practice of driven shooting was easier for the sportsman as he could stand in one place and have birds driven towards him. Pheasants, having been introduced to Britain during the preceding centuries, were found to fly higher and more challengingly than partridge and so they began to find favour on the sporting estate until eventually, they overtook the English partridge in popularity. To maintain their numbers, however, it was necessary to begin rearing stock in order to satisfy the demand – and so the role of the gamekeeper was born.

An unknown keeper wearing attire typical of the period 1870–80. It is interesting to note that all early pictures of keepers tend to be posed in a studio like this one, as due to the constraints of photography at that time, very few photographs were taken out of doors (photo courtesy David S. D. Jones).

Important – but unpopular!

Gamekeepers became very important people in the country hierarchy and, due to the fact that they were providing their employer and his friends with sport, often had the undivided attention of the landowner, making the keeper very unpopular in certain quarters, notably with farming tenants who would have to undertake farming practices more beneficial to game birds than they were to commercial agricultural production.

Village inhabitants would also be wary of the keeper who had immense power and could see that you got into trouble (or even in court) were you to do anything likely to upset his carefully reared and released pheasant stocks.

'Old Velveteens'

Many estate gamekeepers were given their own livery, often of a moleskin-like material which earned them the nick-name of 'Old Velveteens'.

As to their duties, keepers would, with the aid of broody hens, carefully concocted foods and 24-hour protection on the rearing field, rear pheasants from eggs to the age of six weeks before carefully releasing them into suitable woodland. This woodland was, on occasions, specifically planted for game, but existing stands of timber were not forgotten and were improved by the creation of rides, the inclusion of hazel, and low shrubs which produced berries as winter food.

Predator control was also an important part of the gamekeeper's life and anything that might have a detrimental effect on the well-being of game was either shot, trapped or poisoned, thus supposedly ensuring that wild game had a good chance of surviving being hatched in a field bottom and that reared stock would reach maturity.

Keepers and under-keepers on a rearing field of 1899. In those days, there was no option but to hatch game eggs under broody chickens and this shows such birds being let off the nest for their early morning feed (photo courtesy David S. D. Jones).

The Modern Approach

Today's gamekeepers are more enlightened and responsible regarding what constitutes a predator and in their ways of dealing with them. Gamekeeping techniques have also changed: quad-bikes, tractors and 4x4s have replaced the need for the keeper to walk everywhere, or to use a pony and cart to transport birds, equipment and food out to where they were needed on the shoot.

Scientifically formulated compound crumbs and pellets have usurped the secret recipes manufactured on a daily basis by the Victorian and Edwardian keepers, and modern incubators and brooding equipment mean that one person can, if necessary, rear several thousand poults to maturity without the need for a single broody hen.

Mobile phones and emails are nowadays essential in ordering food and contacting beaters, pickers-up and other shoot helpers as the season approaches, and advances in veterinary science have produced medications and hygiene products totally unknown to the early keeper.

Various bodies exist to look after the interests of the gamekeeping and shooting individual, perhaps most notably, the British Association for Shooting and Conservation (BASC), the Countryside Alliance, National Gamekeepers' Organisation (NGO) and National Organisation of Beaters and Pickers Up ('NOBs').

Adapting to change

Today's gamekeepers, professional or amateur, must learn to adapt and to deal with new pressures that are placed upon them. For example, whilst keepers have always

had to contend to a lesser or greater degree with diseases on the rearing field and in the release pens, it is only recently that avian influenza, for example, has become a real potential problem.

In a litigious society, it is also necessary to worry about completing risk assessments, and to spell out the obvious to those participating in a day's shooting in order to avoid the possibility of being sued as a result of a beater tripping over

Today's gamekeepers, professional or amateur, have to deal with pressures unknown to their forebears. They do though, have the advantage of technology: radios, for example, are carried by most on a shooting day but sometimes nothing can beat the old-fashioned notebook and pencil!

barbed wire or cutting his thumb on the edge of a particularly sharp leaf of maize
– and, lest you think I exaggerate, both are true examples. Thankfully though,
despite the world economic worries that exist at the time this book is being written,
many of the large, commercially run shoots still keep going under the watchful eyes
of professional gamekeepers.

Just as many are, however, peopled by enthusiastic amateurs who, by renting
small parcels of land on the outskirts of the bigger shoots, or from interested
farmers, manage to keep the art of gamekeeping very much alive. The latter are run
mainly on a DIY basis by a group of enthusiastic and like-minded friends, who quite
often carry out the keepering duties on a rota system. In other cases, members might
employ a part-time gamekeeper throughout the year or full-time between the busy
months of July and January.

No matter how they are formulated, every one of these shoots and those
involved in their smooth running has always made a significant contribution to the
British countryside and it is to help ensure their continuation that this book has
been written.

≈≈≈

CHAPTER 1

Keepering in the 21st Century

Before going any further, it is as well to establish exactly what a gamekeeper does – there is the oft-quoted 'he walks about with a dog and gun all day' but nothing can be further from the truth!

Although most reading this book will be concerned only with low-ground gamekeeping, and therefore interested mainly in rearing pheasants and partridge, it is, nevertheless, useful to know something of the work of the grouse moor keeper employed in some of the more remote parts of the UK.

What the Grouse Moor Keeper Does

The 'Glorious Twelfth' (12th August) heralds the start of perhaps the rarest and most prestigious of shooting seasons. Grouse shooting is considered by many to be the ultimate sport – and people pay highly for the opportunity. Unlike low-ground shooting, grouse stocks cannot be practically reared and so the success (or failure!) of the grouse moor keeper's work is, quite literally, in the lap of the gods.

The grouse keeper's responsibilities

There is, unfortunately, little one can do about the weather and a cold spell in the spring when the grouse are nesting could have disastrous consequences. A brief resume of the keeper's responsibilities will give you some idea as to what might be involved:

• Arguably, the most important work of the grouse moor keeper will be to cull some of the predators that may harm the nesting hen and her chicks. It is essential that predator control is carried out throughout the year and on most moors will include some form of fox management, the use of box-traps or tunnel traps for stoats, and Larsen traps for the crows.

• Heather burning is also crucial in order to create suitable nesting and feeding areas, but burning can only be legally carried out at certain times of the year and if the weather is particularly bad, then the burning programme may have to be curtailed.

- Strange though it might seem when, to the casual observer, a moor seems to consist of very little else but rocks and stones, some moors need a regular supply of grit placed in strategic areas. Like all birds, having no teeth, grouse need grit to grind down food in the gizzard, thereby aiding digestion: if there is not the right kind of hard flint grit available, the keeper needs to make sure that it is provided artificially and on a regular basis.

- New butts need building and old ones repairing. Sheep find that a line of grouse butts make an ideal shelter from the weather and will rub against some, causing damage to any of the less well-built. The butts on many moors are topped off with turfs of heather and while some will take root there and grow season after season, others will need replacing on an annual basis.

- The 'right to roam' and public access onto moorland areas in some parts of the British Isles can give the grouse moor keeper something of a headache. There are the obvious problems of wandering dogs and heavy-booted feet disturbing or damaging nests – as well as the less obvious ones of a carelessly dropped cigarette butt setting fire to several hundred acres of heather.

Deciding the shape and size of heather to be burnt

Grouse moor keepers have their own ideas regarding the ideal size and shape of burnt patches – some thinking 'squares' to be the best while others prefer long narrow strips. Either way, the moor must contain a good diversification of heather. It is not, however, simply a case of throwing down a match and standing well back: a party of helpers consisting of keepers and local shepherds from the neighbouring moors needs to be organised and wind directions taken into consideration if an out of control fire is to be avoided.

There is the potential for conflict between the keepers and hill farmers, the latter of whom would often like to burn greater areas of heather in order to provide more grazing for their sheep. An over-burned moor over-stocked with sheep can cause problems for the keeper, as both scenarios lessen the potential for grouse feeding and increase the risk of disease.

An important part of the moor keeper's work is the construction and maintenance of the butts from which the Guns shoot – and to continually improve heather growth by means of judicious periodic burning. This particular moor has obviously not been over-grazed by sheep, a vital factor of grouse management.

Might the grouse become our national bird?

In summer 2011, Patrick Mercer, MP for Newark, laid down an Early Day Motion for the red grouse to be accorded the status of our national bird.

This House notes that there has never been an officially recognized bird of the UK ... the native Red Grouse is the only bird on this planet which exclusively inhabits the heather moors of England, Scotland, Wales and Ireland; [and This House] believes that a national bird will generate a wide range of self-sustaining benefits in the environmental, civic, commercial and tourist sectors; [and] affirms that for the Red Grouse to be credibly, authoritatively and permanently appointed as the UK's national bird the Government needs officially to recognize it as such; and duly calls on the Government to endorse the UK National Bird Campaign.

Looking After the Lowland Shoot

It is in connection with low-ground shooting estates that things have changed most significantly over recent years – in fact, in the last decade or so, there have probably been more developments affecting this type of keepering than at any other time. This includes the development of new and very necessary medicines and the banning of old ones; health and safety requirements; the need to attend courses in order to use chainsaws and handle/sell dead game; and the 2004 Hunting Act which curtails some previously allowed and humanely accepted methods of predator control (see Chapter 4 'Predators and Relevant Legislation').

What the pheasant and partridge keeper does
Here, in abbreviated form, are just some of his likely responsibilities:

- At the end of the shooting season, some keepers will be expected to catch up potential laying hens and a few good quality cock birds for stock – these will then be housed in an appropriate laying pen.

- It being a relatively quiet time in the keeper's calendar, every opportunity should be taken to organise a (legal) spring-time offensive against predators which might be harmful to wild bird stocks during the natural nesting season.

- The collecting and hatching of fertile eggs comes next, closely followed by the rearing of chicks – an occupation that will last until mid-summer when poults will need to be taken to the rearing pens.

Weighing up the 'pros and cons' of rearing from day-old

Finance is often the deciding factor when it comes to catching up and rearing one's own birds. Many shoots nowadays think it more economical to buy in their young stock from a game farmer than have to feed laying birds and maintain incubators and rearing equipment. There are definitely several advantages to this, not least the fact that one can order exactly the numbers of birds one intends releasing rather than having to hatch more than one wants in order to ensure that inevitable rearing field losses are covered.

Also, if you have pheasant and partridge poults on the rearing field 'ready to go', you are compelled to release them irrespective of a spell of bad weather; if you buy your birds from a game farm and you have established a good relationship with the owner, they will most likely hang onto your allocation until the weather improves.

DIY syndicates might also consider the practicalities of buying poults rather than considering hatching and rearing from existing stock left after the season: financially, it might turn out to be the best bet – and for practical reasons (there being no full-time keeper to see to everything on a daily basis), it most surely will.

- Whenever there is a spare moment, the gamekeeper must prepare the release pens and improve the habitat so as to encourage birds to stay at home rather than wander off the estate.

- Depending on the type of shooting ground, it might also be necessary to include a few crops of game cover – this will necessitate negotiations with either the local farmer or an agricultural contractor (or, most likely, both).

- Regular, daily feeding is a must – even at the end of the season, adult birds need food … and young stock most certainly will.

- No matter whether on the grouse moors or a lowland shoot, every gamekeeper needs to liaise with potential beaters, pickers-up and other casual shoot helpers prior to the season. The lowland keeper (the ground for which he is responsible being generally of less acreage) will also need to communicate with any neighbours in order to ensure that shooting days are not likely to cause any upset.

Job Opportunities

When I first became interested in keepering in the late 1960s, it was still possible to turn to the classified section of any shooting magazine at the end of the shooting

Regular daily feeding is, although time-consuming, one of the main duties of the lowground keeper ... it begins as soon as the poults arrive in the release pen and must continue into the following spring.

season and view several pages of job offers. You could, within reason, pick and choose from a selection of head-keepers', under-keepers' and beat-keepers' positions being advertised and, what is more, find a position in a part of the UK that best suited you either for topographical or family reasons.

How things have changed in the intervening years and on the rare occasions when a job is advertised, it will be chased by literally hundreds of applicants. Whilst some will be successful in their application, it has to be said that a fair proportion of any jobs advertised in the press will be filled by word of mouth rather than as a result of a written letter of reply.

To ensure you stand the best possible chance of getting an interview, a few brief pointers might be of assistance.

- Take every opportunity to help out on a local shoot whenever possible: contacts and possible referees are all-important.

- Contact agricultural colleges and explore the possibilities of enrolling on one of their gamekeeping courses: on its own, a certificate might not get you a job, but the fact that you have a qualification will help a prospective employer when selecting candidates for interview.

• Think laterally: although you may not want a long-term career in forestry, for example, any experience gained by doing so will undoubtedly help when applying for a keeping job in the future.

• A full-time position might be your ultimate goal, but don't dismiss the opportunity to take up a part-time position and supplement the wages with those from other forms of employment.

• Join the National Gamekeepers' Organisation: there are occasionally jobs offered on their website by, and to, members and even if not, their knowledge and expertise can be a huge help in more general terms.

Gaining practical experience: visit your local shoot

Gaining practical experience prior to considering a college course is important – but how do you go about doing so? Single-handed gamekeepers nowadays have to do the work of several people

---

Some useful organisations

I mentioned above the National Gamekeepers' Organisation. To paraphrase what they nowadays say on television and radio about various products, 'other organisations are available'! Please consider joining, not only the NGO, but also one or more of the following:

• British Association for Shooting and Conservation (BASC)
• Countryside Alliance
• Game & Wildlife Conservation Trust (GWCT)
• Gamekeepers' Welfare Trust (GWT)
• National Organisation of Beaters and Pickers Up (NOBs)
• Scottish Gamekeepers Association (SGA)
• Scottish Association for Country Sports (SACS)
• Union of Country Sports Workers (UCSW)

---

and, even though one person can, with modern equipment, carry out chores which would, a few decades ago, have necessitated two or more, it's rare to find any keeper, professional or amateur, who will not appreciate a helping hand at some time.

For most, it will be their family whose assistance is invaluable when young poults need shutting in for the night, or when birds have begun straying from the release pens and need some judicious dogging-in.

It is, however, not only members of the family who can help out – a team of willing assistants can be extremely advantageous to the shoot, not only during the 'close' season, but perhaps even more so when it comes to organising drives, teams of pickers-up and a multitude of other unseen jobs necessary for the smooth running of the day. Should you be thinking of a gamekeeping career yourself, your assistance will go a long way towards gaining practical experience.

Right: Joining the beating team of a local shoot is a good way for youngsters with an ambition to become gamekeepers to gain some practical experience – and make those all-important contacts.

College Courses

Some agricultural colleges dotted around the British Isles offer full-time residential courses that cover game and wildlife management. They have the facilities and tutoring staff available to ensure training to an industry standard and might offer a variety of possibilities ranging from BTEC Diplomas (for students from the age of 16) right up to BSc Degrees.

Approaching colleges and seeing what's available
Your first and most obvious move will be to contact your nearest agricultural college and see what, if anything, they have to offer. While they might not have a full-time course spanning a year (or more), they could, nevertheless, provide a venue and the use of their facilities to shooting/gamekeeping-based organisations which periodically run short courses.

• The internet will prove useful in finding contact details of your local college – as well as a search engine into which you could just type 'full-time gamekeeping courses' in order to see what comes up on screen.

• All colleges will require you to fill in an application form and to attend an interview. Most will also require that you have at least a modicum of basic experience, whether it be as a result of helping out voluntarily on a rural estate, or by being a regular part of your local shoot and its smooth running (see above: 'Gaining practical experience').

- You can get fully qualified in gamekeeping through an apprenticeship or NVQ course. Many colleges offer these courses where you are assessed in the workplace as well as through written work. You may need to attend college once a week throughout term time but most of your studying and learning is done 'on the job'.

The Lantra Awards Scheme

Lantra, based at Lantra House, Stoneleigh Park, Coventry CV8 2LG, Tel: 02476 419 703, Email: awards@lantra-awards.co.uk) organise many courses and work placements, including several directly pertaining to gamekeeping. Lantra Awards are nationally recognised and are approved to develop and accredit qualifications such as NVQ/SVQ and VRQ by Ofqual and other regulatory bodies. They say that their aim is 'to build a robust, credit-based approach to qualification development that can respond to and play a key role in the development of the Qualification and Credit Framework initiative'.

Short Courses

Once you start looking, it is surprising what is available in the way of short courses and training days. Some of these are essential to the experienced keeper who needs to remain up-dated, useful to the amateur and DIY shoot member or, as in the first possibility to be mentioned below, a potential lifeline to parents worried about their child's future.

More fun than school!

For school children aged 14–16, particularly those with special educational needs, there are relevant short-time courses run by various organisations (such as the Countryside Alliance which, for example, operates a Fishing for Schools project) which aim to provide education in accordance with the Award Scheme Development and Accreditation Network (ASDAN) recognised by the government. The scheme operates in many schools and educational centres (it is listed as one of the few major routes for developing and accrediting wider key skills) and can contribute towards the Certificate of Personal Effectiveness, which is a GCSE alternative for many children.

Although not a direct means of getting into gamekeeping, a course of this nature might just provide youngsters who love the countryside and who are bored by conventional education with sufficient enthusiasm and incentive to consider a worthwhile rural career.

Taking advantage of college workshops

Some agricultural colleges also offer 'workshops' – the subject for which might well be gamekeeping. One such place is Moulton College near Northampton where their 'Wilson Countryside Management Centre', which officially opened in summer

2011, offers workshops on all manner of opportunities, including fish rearing and gamekeeping. Brief classroom lectures are usually augmented with outdoor, hands-on practical experience.

Game-handling courses

Since 2006, when new EU food hygiene regulations came into force, many gamekeepers have had to attend a game-handling course. Basically, the legislation applies to all people who sell game and venison – although they do not apply to those who shoot purely for their own consumption, or occasionally give game away to friends or neighbours.

To check whether you might need to attend such a course, contact or look at the websites of the BASC, NGO, Lantra, or the Royal Society for the Promotion of Health, all of which also organise regular courses throughout the UK.

Courses in chainsaw handling

Modern keepers use much modern equipment – therefore you need to know how to use it safely and correctly. Chainsaws in particular are potentially dangerous machines and so if you use one as a work tool, it is essential that you have received the proper training. Lantra Awards, along with some private forestry organisations, offer a variety of chainsaw training courses – arguably, the most suitable of which as far as the gamekeeper is concerned, might be one of their Integrated Training and Assessment (ITA) courses, which lead to a Certificate of Training.

If you want to find out more about chainsaw handling, the Health and Safety Executive have a very comprehensive and useful leaflet available. A copy of *Chainsaws at Work* can be obtained from HSE Books, PO Box 1999, Sudbury, Suffolk CO10 2WA, Tel: 01787 881165, Fax: 01787 313995, Website: www.hsebooks.co.uk (HSE priced publications are also available from bookshops and free leaflets can be downloaded from HSE's website: www.hse.gov.uk).

A training course for part-time keepers

As the Game Conservancy, what is now known as the Game and Wildlife Conservation Trust (GWCT) always ran courses for full and part-time gamekeepers at their headquarters in Fordingbridge, Hampshire. Nowadays, they regularly organise a three-day residential course which, they say, 'enables participants to keep abreast of current management practices and legislation'.

Aside from practical direct gamekeeping advice, the courses cover topics such as deer management, shoot economics and flight pond construction. If you are a farmer running a part-time shoot or at all involved in any way with a small shooting syndicate, such a course would be well worth attending. If, on the other hand, you are a full-time, professional keeper, the GWCT periodically run one-day courses at various estates up and down the country.

Gamekeeping awareness days

Training days set up by the British Association for Shooting and Conservation

Mike Short of the Game & Wildlife Conservation Trust updating keepers in predator control techniques (photo courtesy of Peter Thompson/GCWT).

(BASC) for part-time and amateur keepers are always fully attended and give the participants plenty of opportunity to learn about game management.

The days involve no Power-point presentations or tests – simply the chance to spend the day on a small shoot in the company of experienced gamekeepers looking at all aspects of their daily duties. It is also a good opportunity to ask questions and get some useful hints and tips.

Deer management courses

Training is a legal and essential part of deer stalking and management, with national qualifications: DSC Level One and DSC Level Two. Several organisations, such as the British Deer Society, the BASC and the Saint Hubert Club of Great Britain, are authorised to deliver and supervise these training qualifications. They also run courses for the more experienced stalker and deer manager.

A useful book

In autumn 2011, the British Deer Society produced a new book providing information on detecting health conditions and anomalies, common parasites and diseases amongst British deer. The guide is ideal for stalkers taking the DSC1 and DSC2 and the Large Game Hygiene Certificate. *The Field Guide to Diseases and Conditions of Wild Deer* in the UK is endorsed by a number of organisations including BASC, the Deer Initiative, the NGO and Scottish Natural Heritage. A spiral-bound, pocket-sized book with informative text and colour photographs throughout, it is waterproof and tear resistant – so ideal to take outdoors. To find out more, visit www.bds.org.uk or telephone 01425 655434.

The Shoot Benchmarking Survey

In 2010, the land agents Smiths Gore (in association with GunsOnPegs, shoot letting agents) inaugurated their 'Benchmarking Survey'. A refined and improved survey was launched in January 2011, the results of which make fascinating reading and are of value to every shoot, commercial or private, large or small. Hopefully, this will become an annual publication.

Some interesting findings

Dealing mainly with costings – a vital part of any shooting venture – the data of the last available survey seem to indicate that, from a sample of over 100 shoots that rear and release game and employ a gamekeeper, non-commercial shoots had an average daily bag of around 110 birds, whilst commercial sporting estates were slightly less than double that figure.

A six-week old poult bought in for the season 2010/11 cost between £3.43 and £3.78 on average, and the average salary for a gamekeeper was, at the lowest end of the scale, £13,000 and, at the highest, £18,555. In addition to their fiscal wages, keepers generally receive some or all of the following:

- house
- utility bills
- vehicle
- dog allowance
- clothing allowance
- mobile phone
- other benefits.

NB: In the Benchmarking Survey, headkeepers were, as might be expected, paid a higher salary and were given a greater percentage of the above than other categories of keepers.

Tied houses are a part of many employment packages. Not all gamekeepers' cottages will be as idyllic as this one – but a great many are.

CHAPTER 2

Gamekeepers as Managers

Gamekeeping helps to ensure a balanced countryside with plentiful wildlife. However, with recent developments, you now need a far wider range of skills and knowledge, any of which might include the following:
• an appreciation of current agricultural/forestry policy
• environmental legislation
• use of prescription-only veterinary medication (POM-Vs)
• business management.

So, not only do today's gamekeepers need to have an understanding of the countryside and an empathy with the game bird stocks and wild fauna for which they are responsible, they are also increasingly becoming shoot managers accountable for the letting of days, annual budgets and the sourcing of materials and sub-contractors.

Managing the Countryside

Just what you can do to improve the habitat on your particular shoot is discussed in the next chapter, but it is worth considering the benefits that occur nationwide as a result of your efforts. Some research by the BASC showed that gamekeepers manage around 7.3 million hectares of land in the UK – which is, unbelievably, an area almost the size of Scotland.

'Unsung heroes of conservation'
The first ever national survey of Britain's gamekeepers (published in 2011) was carried out by the Game & Wildlife Conservation Trust (GWCT) and revealed the key role keepers play in conserving wildlife and habitats across the country. Nearly 1,000 keepers took part and the area of land managed by them (1,337,454 hectares) was five times the total area of all Britain's National Nature Reserves (255,789 hectares) and 13 times the total area of all Royal Society for Protection of Birds (RSPB) reserves (101,581 hectares).

The survey, entitled 'Gamekeepers and Wildlife', prompted Lindsay Waddell, chairman of the National Gamekeepers' Organisation, to say in a press release that, 'The truth is that gamekeepers undoubtedly host more wildlife on their land than all the other nature conservation bodies put together'.

Gamekeeping and the Rural Economy

Exact figures vary depending on whom you talk to, but generally, it is accepted that there are almost three-quarters of a million people who participate regularly in some form of game shooting. Their interest brings in all manner of revenue. It might be incidental in the form of purchasing cartridges, clothing or even dog-food for their pampered pooch. More importantly though, their direct input in the shape of syndicate fees and/or purchase of shooting days (and subsequent employment of gamekeepers) is often essential in helping to maintain a particular estate's overall financial viability.

With this in mind, you need to work closely with any agricultural and forestry enterprises in order to achieve workable management policies which are both economically viable and beneficial to the well-being of game and wildlife.

There can be no doubt that ground that has been managed with game and shooting in mind will greatly benefit wildlife in general. On this particular North Yorkshire estate, valleys and undulating countryside in the foreground lead off to prestigious grouse moors on the horizon (photo courtesy of Swinton Park).

Renting Ground

Professional gamekeepers are, of course, generally employed by existing landowners and have no need to consider the possibility of having to rent ground. A few reading this will, however, be considering the subject of gamekeeping as a result of being a member of a DIY syndicate where everyone is responsible for at least a part of the shoot's success. Before that happens though, you might need to consider finding land over which to shoot – this bit is for you!

Some possibilities to consider

It used to be an easy matter to rent shooting on Forestry Commission ground and, provided that one abided by the conditions laid out on the contract and sent in an annual return form, you were left pretty much to your own devices.

In the southern region alone, the letting of sporting rights still generates over half a million pounds each year, but the actual price per hectare depends on what part of the country you live (and also fluctuates in some regions because of demand). Thus it might be possible to find a potential shoot costing only a few pounds per hectare in Scotland whereas in the south-east the price per hectare is considerably more.

Like many countryside enterprises, there is a very valid need for each area to diversify and increase their potential revenue by whatever means possible. Rambling trails, off-road cycling and café franchises all bring in people and much-needed cash, but such activities do, inevitably, curtail the possibility of shooting and stalking tenancies becoming available due to the obvious safety aspect and conflict of interests.

Renting from private sources

Probably far easier said than done, it is, nevertheless, sometimes possible to rent land from private owners – at a cost. Occasionally shoots to rent appear in the classified sections of either the sporting press or farming magazines, but it is only occasionally. It could also be worth a phone call to your regional offices of national land agents such as Smiths Gore who may, if you're very fortunate, know of some land to rent.

What's the best approach?

A direct approach is often best: a visit to the estate office which controls an existing shoot might result in the offer of some boundary land which, although of no value to the main shoot, could provide you, as a part of a small DIY syndicate, with exactly what you're looking for. You will, however, need to be prepared to release game yourself as the members of the main shoot will not be too happy to think of you shooting 'their' birds which have wandered over onto your land!

Approaching a local farmer could work well. In return for becoming a member of your syndicate or being given a couple of days' free shooting, he may be prepared to come to some arrangement over his land.

It is accepted that there are almost three-quarters of a million people who participate regularly in some form of game shooting. Their interest brings in all manner of revenue and is therefore vital to the rural economy.

Selling Your Sport

You might nowadays be responsible for selling a day or two's shooting to offset costs (not something gamekeepers of Edwardian times ever needed to consider!) and so a few pointers as to how this could be achieved might just prove useful.

• Offering your clients a great service begins well before the shooting day and you must make sure that you convey a professional, business-like approach at all times.

• Anyone selling a shooting at whatever level must look after the client. You are your own biggest marketing asset and how you interact with the customer at the outset will affect whether they book and, more importantly, whether or not they will return.

• Place adverts in the obvious places: notably, the sporting/shooting press.

Use the services of an agent: there are plenty around who are geared up to selling shooting and will, most likely, have possible clients ready and waiting – freeing you to simply provide the required day's sport!

What happens when things go wrong?
On a let day, a team of Guns should have previously stipulated their requirements and negotiated a fee (usually on a per bird basis) beforehand. Always ask for a deposit when the day is booked and the balance six weeks before the proposed day's shooting.

If, at the end of the day, the bag is much smaller than advertised, you might need to give the Guns a percentage of their money back, or offer them another day. If the numbers are only slightly down, say 150 on a 200 bird day shoot, most will accept the shortfall, particularly if they've seen some good high flying birds – after all, they come along for the quality of sport, friendship and a day out.

It always pays to have someone, either on the game cart or in the picking-up team, who uses a 'clicker' to count the number of cartridges fired. If necessary, this can be compared against the number of birds shot – 1-in-3 is average for a good team of Guns, but again, it will depend on the height and quality of birds.

Getting On with the Shoot Manager

Many years ago, all shooting decisions would have been made by discussions between the gamekeeper and the landowner; nowadays though, it is increasingly likely that the shoot will have another person in charge.

Sometimes this might be someone already employed by the estate or rental agency. It might also be a shooting tenant, and even the small friendly DIY syndicate should agree that at least one of its members is there to take charge and responsibility.

Whatever title they are given, be it shoot captain or shoot manager, it is essential that they have an understanding of the sport and a good working relationship with the gamekeeper or person accepted to be in control of the day-to-day running of the shoot and on a shooting day itself.

• Both should have a good knowledge of shooting and instil confidence in one another and everyone else.

• A good shoot manager and keeper should be able to talk to people and explain what will happen throughout the day and on each drive.

• They will pre-plan, well before the season, the numbers reared, siting of game crops, advertising of 'let' days, etc.

• Get on well with any tenant farmers and neighbours – you can only do this by earning their respect.

- Know the ground well – the directions woods are to be driven, the positioning of Gun pegs, how to get from A to B without getting lost or a vehicle stuck.

- Discuss the drives either the night before or on the morning of the shoot. Take into consideration weather conditions and likely wind directions.

A good shoot manager should be able to talk to people and explain what will happen throughout the day and on each drive – and still have time for a laugh and a joke! (photo courtesy of Elliot Hobson).

Holding the Purse Strings

Gamekeepers are, as we have seen, nowadays often responsible for implementing an annual budget – and seeing that it is adhered to! As a typical modern keeper, you might be expected to be in charge of:

- Setting the annual budget (taking into account fixed and variable costs) and having it approved by either your employer or all the other DIY syndicate members.

- The purchase of one-off capital equipment (usually offset over five years or more) such as vehicles, rearing equipment and the like.

- Paying any rent on land not owned by the shoot.

- Negotiating a deal with agricultural contractors for any necessary game crops, making sure that you include the cost of seed and fertiliser etc. within the price rather than, as sometimes happens, being presented with an extra, unexpected bill after planting.

- Finding the best deal for crumbs and pellets. In this case, the cheapest might not be the best as, to keep prices down, the percentage of vital ingredients such as protein might be less – you should always compare the various manufacturers' lists of nutritional contents as well as their prices.

- Employing and paying the beaters and other shoot helpers.

- Organising outside caterers for the shoot lunch.

- Setting the price per bird shot figure (having taken into consideration all the likely out-goings) on shoots which sell days or have a paying syndicate.

Public accounts

Perhaps the strangest question I've ever been asked (by a journalist, so perhaps that explains it!) concerning managing a shoot in the twenty-first century was whether or not shoot accounts should ever be made public. Why? They are a matter for the estate. Some shoots will undoubtedly be liable for VAT and will have to produce accounts for this reason, but I cannot see any reason why they should ever have to come into the public domain.

Regular syndicate members may wish to see a set of accounts that take into consideration the running expenses of the year such as wages, transport costs, cost of birds, rearing and releasing, feed, capital equipment, etc., but that's as far as it should go.

The modern day keeper cannot spend all his hours outdoors (much as he might like to!) and will, in addition, need to spend some time at his desk sorting out all manner of shoot paperwork, making phone calls and ordering equipment, stock and food.

Being the 'Public Face' of Gamekeeping

Your management skills can be put to good use in some unusual ways. For many generations, gamekeepers have been thought of as being quite reclusive but it's nowadays a valuable asset to be a good 'people person'.

There are a number of reasons for this, not least the fact that keepers need to be seen in a good light at all times. With that in mind, it is up to you to put actual facts forward – and dispel any commonly held myths. Some of the ways you can do this are by:

• Joining the NGO and suggesting that you become a spokesperson for your area. You will then be the one to be contacted by the local media and invited to comment on any related issues before they make the headlines.

• Volunteering to give talks to local groups such as the Women's Institute, local rambling clubs and conservation societies.

• Inviting schools to visit your estate (you will need to fill in a risk assessment in conjunction with the teacher in charge) so that the pupils (and their teachers) can see exactly what it is gamekeepers do. This can have at least two positive outcomes:
    – Children are informed first-hand rather than picking up any preconceptions from others.
    – Those most stimulated by their visit might eventually decide to take up gamekeeping – or at least become enthusiastic members of the beating team.
• Offering to write a regular column for your parish or village magazine. Blatant propaganda it might be, but you will at least have the opportunity to point out why dogs should be kept under control in the nesting season and ask for public cooperation on a shooting day with regards to wandering from footpaths and other rights-of-way.

Managing Your Temper!

Approaching a member of the public who is somewhere they shouldn't be on the shoot can go two ways! You are, though, more likely to get their cooperation by starting your conversation with something along the lines of, 'Hallo – you look as if you might be lost' rather than being openly aggressive.

Much depends on the situation in which you find them and, if they've discovered a Larsen trap of yours, for example, you might well be accused of cruelty – or worse. Explaining the trap's purpose, the fact that it is perfectly legal and that, in catching crows and magpies, you are helping the survival of the songbird population as well as game, might well help diffuse the situation.

Whatever happens, if you lose your temper you will undoubtedly alienate that person and also have done gamekeeping a great disservice.

And finally...

Some of you reading this book might be doing so more out of general interest rather than because of an active desire to be directly involved in gamekeeping. Whilst some of the points raised in this chapter might not therefore apply, you may, nevertheless, be keen on finding a little shooting for yourselves – in which case, it could be worth approaching a farmer and offering to carry out a bit of vermin control on their behalf. Here are some comments to consider when cold-calling in search of 'permission'.

• Remember that, quite rightly in these days of increased rural theft, farmers can be suspicious of 'cold-callers'.

• A lot of farms are already shot over by game shooting syndicates and the like – and so any vermin control will most certainly be carried out during the 'close' season by their members, keeper and/or regular shoot helpers such as beaters.

• Make it clear that you are only interested in shooting vermin (squirrels, rabbits or pigeons) and, if possible, be able to produce references which say you are trustworthy in such situations.

• Look smart and presentable – first impressions do count.

• Learn to accept that, if there is currently no shooting on a farmer's land, there is probably a good reason for this – some just do not like shooting and what it entails. There is absolutely no point in trying to persuade such a person otherwise and you will only alienate them.

CHAPTER 3

Habitat Management and Improvement

Much of a shoot's success and game holding potential is down to habitat improvement and, as such, is often the responsibility of you, the gamekeeper. Some improvements (the layering of a wind-breaking hedge around woodland, for example) are very obvious, but other examples might not be seen quite so readily.

Big Improvements at Little Cost

A chalk pit or 'dell-hole' which has, for one reason or another, been created in the middle of a field or on the edge of woodland can be used to great advantage. All too often, however, its potential is not seen and over the years, livestock have been allowed access, leaving no under cover or protection from the wind. With a little effort on your part – and often all that involves is the erection of a stock-proof fence – the place could soon become a potentially brilliant drive, especially if it is possible to surround it with a strip of game cover. The sides of the pit will already act as a windbreak and once fenced off, will very quickly thicken up with bramble, creating cover and security for game birds. If you then add a feed hopper or two together with a bale of straw you are almost guaranteed success.

Creating cheap woodlands

It is inevitable that all shoots that are maintained on a long-term basis, will, at

Time isn't necessarily money!

Time and not money need be the only expense on some shoots. Oak saplings can be removed from under the canopy of the parent tree. Either take them home and plant them in a corner of the garden (from where they can be removed and sited on the shoot in five or six years' time) or transplant them directly into similar soil conditions in a more sympathetic part of the wood. Similarly, rather than letting all the self-sown birch and alder survive, if the majority are either dug up or cut down, leaving only the strongest ones to mature, they will, in time, produce a cheap broad-leaved woodland. If a few other, soil compatible species were also introduced, the varied habitat created will eventually be suitable for both game and other incidental flora and fauna.

some stage or another, need to carry out some form of tree planting. It might not be necessary for you to plant a whole new wood, coppice or spinney, but some shrubs for shelter, cover and flushing points will undoubtedly be required at some point.

Birch and alder, in particular, actually do a very good job of planting themselves; producing huge numbers of very small seeds which travel considerable distances and which are likely to fall in places where there are few trees and therefore minimal competition. Once in the soil they grow rapidly and begin to produce new seeds when as little as five years old, thus starting off the cycle again. In contrast, species such as oak produce fewer seeds but the acorns contain lots of food for the developing seedling, giving it a good start in life, particularly if it finds itself under the protective canopy of other trees.

How to go about some general improvements
According to new research by the Game & Wildlife Conservation Trust (GWCT), pheasant releasing is one of the main incentives for managing and planting hedgerows in Britain, thereby conserving a wide range of wildlife. The

A stile, or better still, a securely hinged gate, is a useful addition to any new fencing around a tree plantation, especially if the fencing is built tall enough to offer protection against deer damage – in which case some form of entrance and exit is essential.

Stylish behaviour!

Any recently erected fencing around woodland on the shoot will benefit from the addition of a small stile, over which beaters and Guns can step without pushing down and damaging the netting. Taller deer fencing might cause a bit more of a problem, but in any long length of fencing, there is usually a short horizontal straining bar fixed between the top of two posts, near to which it should be possible to fix two shorter posts either side of the fence and attach a connecting plank between the two, thus forming a simple two-stage stile.

Consider the inclusion of a 'dog-flap' in such fences, but before you do so, make sure you have the permission of whoever is responsible for the fence itself, otherwise they might not be too pleased to see 'adaptations' to their carefully-constructed and expensive fence line.

research also shows that game estates had up to 65 percent more hedgerow per square kilometre than farms with no shooting. Their studies concluded that '...the tendency for wilder hedgebanks and greater hedgerow abundance on game estates is due to the recognition by game managers of the value of hedgerows as habitats for gamebirds'. What more incentive could we need?

Hedgerow know-how
Hedgerows always need managing as they obviously cannot be kept at the perfect level and condition indefinitely. Options include trimming (every two or three years), re-shaping (every decade), layering and coppicing (as and when).

Trimming and re-shaping are self-explanatory. Layering involves partially cutting through each suitable stem and bending and weaving them between thin stakes (usually of hazel) hammered at intervals along the hedge length. Coppicing is far more drastic and requires cutting mature stems to ground level before allowing the resultant stumps to re-grow.

When planting new hedgerows, it can be a problem to know what species to use. As a general rule, either copy the species present in nearby existing hedges, or to differentiate it as a new hedge use a single species such as hawthorn. In both cases the types of saplings or 'whips' used should be common to your particular area.

For more advice, contact the Natural England Enquiry Office (enquiries@hedgelink.org.uk) and ask for a copy of their DVD 'A cut above the rest: managing hedges for the future'. Three leaflets accompany the film, all of which will prove extremely useful.

Rides, trimming and sky-lighting
Further general improvements may include the trimming of existing woodland rides or even the creation of new ones. You might need to utilise a narrow winding ride through the woods as a feeding area, or want to use a wider one as a place to stand your Guns whilst the surrounding cover is being driven. In both cases, the shrubby

---

Grants for hedgerow planting – and more

A grant towards planting hedgerows is available in some parts of the British Isles via the Environmental Stewardship scheme. Some local authorities also have accessible funding for all manner of small-scale tree planting (including hedgerows).

There is also another grant which might prove to be of interest to shoots and gamekeepers, especially if existing woodland has been neglected or 'under-managed'. In 2011, the Forestry Commission and the Country Land & Business Association worked together in order to turn available government cash from Natural England's bio-energy crops scheme into the Woodfuel Woodland Improvement Grant. Woodland and game birds will undoubtedly benefit.

edges will require occasional trimming in order to ensure that the side and overhead canopy do not become overgrown.

For various reasons, it could be beneficial to consider cutting out a small area of mature trees in the centre of a wood – perhaps to allow a little sunlight to penetrate and encourage the growth of additional bramble and understory. Be careful though: athough keepers and foresters of the past could have cut down trees as and where they saw fit, such cavalier behaviour is nowadays frowned upon and often illegal.

Mature trees take minutes to cut down but generations to grow and so, quite rightly, some may be subject to preservation orders, be integral to a forestry programme, or part

Dying, dead or dangerous?

Under the Town and Country Planning Act 1990, the consent of the local planning authority will be required to cut down or carry out work on any trees that are subject to a preservation order or are in a designated conservation area. Damaging or destroying a protected tree is a criminal offence, unless it is dying, dead or dangerous. If the tree is felled, a suitable replacement must generally be planted as soon as is reasonably possible.

Keeping wide woodland rides in good order helps create natural flushing points, breaks in large areas of trees, easy access for shoot vehicles and perfect places on which to position a team of Guns whilst game is being driven towards them.

of a government payment scheme. Depending on your particular location and circumstances, check with the landowner, agent, the relevant section of your local council or, for definitive legal advice, the Tree Council or Natural England.

Planting New Woodlands

The Woodland Creation Grant organised by the Forestry Commission might just prove of interest to those in the fortunate position of having unused land which could usefully be planted up with trees.

The scheme pays up to £1,800 per hectare, subject to a scoring system, where various criteria such as size, wildlife, landscape and public benefit are assessed. An additional contribution of up to £2,000 per hectare is paid where applicants meet national or regional priorities such as biodiversity and public access – two criteria that do not necessarily conflict with shooting activities and habitat improvements. For more information on the scheme, visit: www.forestry.gov.uk/ewgs-wcg

Without official permission and a valid felling permit, you are likely to be breaking the law if you just decide to take matters into your own hands and remove mature trees on a whim. Check with the relevant authorities before even considering using a chainsaw anywhere near such trees!

Ponds and Pond Construction

Logically, the summer would be a good time to consider such a project as, given normal weather, the ground should be dry enough to allow access for heavy machinery whilst still being soft enough to dig.

Constructing a new pond from scratch is an exciting project, but an expensive one, so it is important that you consider exactly what is required before going ahead. Obviously designs differ depending on its eventual use – a trout pond, for example, would need to be some 2.5m deep in places, whereas a sanctuary for dabbling ducks such as mallard might be sufficient at only a few inches in depth. A duck pond will feel more secure to flighting birds if it has a screen of trees.

Some important considerations

Islands, feeding bays, the height of dams, type of soil being used to line the pond, water outlets and even, as the French do, a bank-side area set aside for the growing of a small crop on which the ducks will feed, all need careful consideration. When constructing new ponds, ground conditions will not always retain water; however,

A series of small flight ponds will, in most cases, be better than one large expanse of water. For mallard and other dabbling ducks, the pond depth need not be very much at all but if you're hoping to encourage divers, a metre or more will be necessary.

with a new range of products that are now available, this problem can perhaps be overcome by the use of heavy duty liners – provided, of course, that you are not intending your pond to be so big that the size makes doing so prohibitively expensive or impractical.

If you are intending to construct a large pond with a surface area over a certain size (and this may vary depending on where you are in the country), local water authorities will need to be consulted, planning permission sought and dams built to particular dimensions. To be sure you do not fall foul of any of this, it is worth contacting the Environment Agency for further advice.

Clearing Undesirable Vegetation

Japanese knotweed

Japanese knotweed (*Fallopia japonica*) is, in the twenty-first century, causing damage to both fisheries and duck flighting lakes, as well as to the whole countryside in general. Amazingly, it will regenerate from pieces as small as 2cm in soil or in water and, in the UK, this weed is one of a number listed under Schedule 9 of the Wildlife and Countryside Act 1981, it being an offence in the UK to plant it or otherwise cause it to grow. It can be effectively eradicated by repeated cutting and burning. Depending on exactly where it is growing, it might also be possible to rotovate the root system, which should be raked and burnt in situ, thereby avoiding possible repercussions under the Wildlife and Countryside Act which also states that it is an offence to transport Japanese knotweed.

Ragwort

Ragwort is a toxic plant which poses a threat to many forms of livestock (although deer are supposedly less prone to its ill effects than are domestic livestock). The Weeds Act 1959 and the Ragwort Control Act 2003 merely give local authorities the power to order its control in specific areas and, contrary to popular opinion, it is not otherwise illegal to have it growing on your land.

Even so, it does no one any good whatsoever and should not be allowed to grow unchecked on the shoot. Likely places where it will grow include areas of release pens which have been taken out of grassland or crop production in order to give the poults a variety of mixed vegetation rather than just woodland cover.

Whilst there are weedkillers which will destroy it, the surest remedy is to pull it up and burn it.

Rhododendrons – good or bad?

A recent project carried out in the New Forest saw rhododendron bushes being grubbed out and burnt due to the fact that it has been discovered that they may harbour parasites harmful to some species of trees. Necessary though the work may eventually prove to be, it is a shame because the dry, friable leaf mould found under clumps of such bushes provides the perfect habitat for several wild birds, most notably woodcock which, in particularly hard weather, use the rhododendron as shelter and for probing into the fallen, rotting leaves in search of insects – perhaps the very ones that the foresters are hoping to eradicate.

Rhododendrons are also useful growing in areas from which pheasants are to be driven and flushed and it's my experience that when a line of beaters come up to such cover, there is an immediate surge of fresh enthusiasm due to the fact that everyone knows there's likely to be at least a couple of birds hiding in there.

Controlling Invasive Bracken

The sale and supply of the herbicide Asulam – a very effective controller of invasive bracken, especially on moorland areas – was made illegal on 31 December 2011 and any stored stocks of the product must be used by 31 December 2012. This is as a result of a decision by an EU Standing Committee on the Food Chain and Animal Health over concerns about the chemical's safety when used on spinach and other food crops. However, the GWCT and other conservation organisations have raised concerns about the ban having huge implications for the future preservation of birds, plants and other rare species, as a result of which they are calling for the ban's reversal.

Bracken is particularly invasive in parts of Scotland – hence the reason that the Scottish NFU is requesting that the UK government allows gamekeepers and landowners to continue using the spray Asulam.

The situation in Scotland

Meanwhile, despite the EU's decision, NFU Scotland is to ask the UK government to allow gamekeepers and landowners to continue using Asulam. If their request to consider issuing a national emergency authorisation for its use is successful, it may allow the product to be available for use for a few months each year (although the conditions of its use would be limited). If you have a particular problem with encroaching bracken, it will pay you to get in touch with DEFRA or your local NFU representative to find out the latest situation.

Improving Your Chances with Wild Partridges

The numbers of wild English partridges declined dramatically towards the end of the last century. Nowadays, thanks to research, good conservation practice and habitat improvement, the future looks much brighter. You can help by creating brood-rearing habitat with plenty of insect food adjacent to good nesting areas, providing seed food through the winter by the planting of wild bird seed game crop mixtures or trying to persuade the farmer to leave some stubble fields over winter.

Provide dust-bathing areas

Dusting sites are essential to partridge and, where these are not plentiful, it is quite a simple matter to provide artificial ones. Here's a three-point construction plan:

1. Firstly, dig out some turf, but do not dig a hole so deep that after a shower of rain it becomes more like a flight pond! It is preferable that all dusting shelters are made to face southwards, thus creating a sun trap and being more protected from the rain and wind.

2. Fill the depression thus made with sand, bonfire ash or even the residue from the household wood burner.

3. The site can then be roofed in with two or three sheets of corrugated iron supported by four corner posts and some cross-members. The height at the front should be around 1m sloping to about half that height at the back. Some people make their shelters by merely laying one end of the sheets on the ground and holding them in place with the soil removed from making the depression. However, if you follow this method, there is a danger that any partridges using the site may, one day, be disturbed by a predator and not be able to escape as quickly as they could if the back was left open.

A gritty subject

Partridges, or any other game bird for that matter, should be able to find their own source of grit which is very necessary for grinding up food as it passes from the crop to the gizzard. Distribute a few piles of mixed grit in prominent places around the shoot – a dusting site would be an obvious choice as would any feeding areas. Although not absolutely essential, the addition of such luxuries all help to ensure the well-being of game and, given a moderate spring and summer, you might well be rewarded with a few wild bird broods as a result (see also the section 'Grit' in Chapter 8).

Farming and partridges

On farmland, do all you can to help wild partridge survival by trying to persuade the farmer responsible to take an interest and adopt one or more of the following suggestions.

- Create conservation headlands and/or grass margins around arable fields as nesting habitat for grey partridges. Include species such as cocksfoot in the seed mix to create tussocks. After the margins are established, cut only in the autumn once every three years. Avoid cutting all margins in the same year.

- Avoid spraying the outer 6m of cereal fields with non-selective insecticides or herbicides (this enables beneficial insects and chick food for grey partridges to survive).

- Spray and cultivate stubbles as late as possible as they provide important winter-feeding habitat.

- Make 'beetle banks' in fields greater than 20ha to provide nesting cover and overwintering habitat for beneficial insects.

- Grow spring-sown arable fodder crops or small plots of wild bird cover in areas that are predominantly agricultural grassland – both the crop and resultant stubble provide abundant seed food.

- Fence off margins of up to 6m around improved grass fields and leave these unfertilised, uncut and ungrazed (some, but not all, should, however, be grazed or cut every two to three years – preferably about September time).

Gamekeepers as Conservationists

There can be no better way to end this chapter than by reminding you again of the important role that the modern gamekeeper plays in countryside conservation. I know I broached the topic briefly at the beginning of the previous chapter, but even so, the fact that so much of what the keeper does as part of his everyday work benefits the natural flora and fauna directly is well worth repetition. It is also a very valid point to raise should you ever become embroiled in a discussion regarding the ethics of shooting!

A hedgerow that runs between two strips of game cover will provide security, shelter, dusting and nesting areas for partridges – but only if it is regularly maintained. As can be seen in this illustration, if left too long, the major components become too tall and straggly (and may even die back) so, whilst there's currently plenty of cover here, things might not be as good in a few years' time.

The NGO is fortunate in having two high-profile celebrities as its patrons and they have done much to make the public understand the conservation work carried out by gamekeepers. In addition to the evocative Foreword written for this book, Alan Titchmarsh also pointed out in a recent magazine interview that:

> *A lot of people think gamekeepering is just about killing, but if you talk to a gamekeeper they are equally, if not more, concerned with preserving nature. These are men more in tune with nature than anybody else and I have a lot of time for them. They are practical countrymen.*

It is also worth noting some of what Professor David Bellamy had to say during the first ever presentation of The Bellamy Trophy – a major new countryside award for conservation and education:

> *Oh, to be a young man again. Looking back I would have loved to have been a gamekeeper. Gamekeepers are real conservationists with a hands-on approach that keeps our countryside alive. The media and the public should sit up, pin back their ears and listen to what gamekeepers have to say. Our*

wildlife needs them. We need them. Gamekeepers are champions of sustainability ... Gamekeepers are close to nature. Down the years, gamekeepers have taught me volumes about the countryside ... I am proud that this award recognises keepers who have gone out of their way to teach others about how the woods and fields should be properly tended. I take my hat off to them all.

Perhaps Alice Barnard, now ex-Chief Executive of the Countryside Alliance, summed it all up in August 2011 when, in that role, she said:

Nowadays everything that is good for the environment is immediately picked up by the Government, given taxpayer subsidy and over-administrated. Yet quietly and consistently, the shooting community is undertaking fantastic conservation work that will benefit Britain and British wildlife for generations to come.

Gamekeepers as diplomats!

Some parts of the estate not used directly for shooting and habitat improvement, whilst not technically a public place, might nevertheless have been enjoyed by locals for many years. Rather than alienate yourself by trying to implement a 'blanket ban', you might like to consider putting up small signs pointing out that, whilst the estate has no objection to locals having access, you would request that it is only for walking by nearby residents and that others should seek written permission. In addition, you might like to say that you would prefer no horse-riders or cyclists used the land – and give your reasons. Point out too that paths can be slippery and you can take no responsibility for any injuries suffered by walkers. Then, as a final touch, apologise for the 'legalese' way in which the note is written. It's my experience that the public appreciate the gesture – and far more importantly, are less likely to wander into more conservation-sensitive parts of your land!

CHAPTER 4

≈≈≈

Predators and Relevant Legislation

Whereas a gamekeeper of Victorian times might legitimately have displayed a gibbet of so-called 'vermin' likely to have destroyed his game stocks in order that his employer could see exactly what he'd been up to (and what he was paying him for), you, as a keeper today – quite rightly – cannot.

Keeper Within the Law

The subject of predator control is a complex one – it always has been, and, as each year passes, it gets even more complicated. If there is one thing likely to cause consternation in the eyes of the general public, it is the subjects covered within this particular chapter. Therefore, no matter how private you think your estate may be, it is essential that whatever you do, in whatever context, is legally, humanely and justifiably acceptable.

The Wildlife and Countryside Act et al.
For a bit of light reading (I joke!), arm yourself with a copy of the Wildlife and Countryside Act 1981 and its various adjuncts. Heavy work though they might be, they will stop you falling foul of the law.

Remember, what might be law in England and Wales could very well vary in Scotland and Northern Ireland. For example, the Wildlife and Natural Environment Bill (NI) was introduced into the NI Assembly in 2010 to amend existing legislation and the resulting Act became law in August 2011.

Being Legal with a Gun

To possess any kind of firearm in the UK, you must have either a shotgun certificate or a firearms certificate issued by your local police authority.

A shotgun is, broadly speaking, a smooth-barrelled gun which discharges a number of pellets (rather than a single slug or bullet) and must not be capable of holding more than three cartridges. The barrel length must be over 61cm.

51

A firearm is, simplistically, any barrelled weapon which is not a shotgun, air-gun or 'prohibited weapon', i.e. in the context of shooting and gamekeeping, a rifle. Known as 'Section 1' firearms, to possess one, you must be able to show the police that you have a 'good reason to possess' and, unlike a shotgun certificate, the firearms certificate only gives authority to hold specific rifles, and the applicant must give good reasons as to the need for each individual one.

The minimum age to apply

A firearms certificate is valid for five years and can be applied for by anyone over the age of 18 who can then buy firearms and ammunition as shown on the certificate. (Persons aged 14–18 may be allowed to possess a firearm but not buy a firearm or ammunition.)

There is, contrary to what some newspapers would have us believe, no legal minimum age limit for anyone applying for a shotgun certificate (although there are restrictions on their use by a minor, just one of which is being supervised by an adult). Once again, a shotgun certificate is valid for five years. Should you have reason to have both firearms and shotguns, it is possible to have what is known as a 'co-terminous' certificate for both.

Where to keep your guns

The precise requirements for the storage of firearms and shotguns are not actually specified in law. However, current legislation states that they 'must be stored securely at all times so as to prevent, so far as is reasonably practicable, access to the guns by unauthorised persons'. In practice – and your local police firearms officer will check during a home visit before recommending that your application be granted – this is likely to be a steel cabinet constructed and certified to comply with BS 7558, rawlbolted to the wall.

Whilst there are no specific

Current legislation states that shotguns and rifles 'must be stored securely at all times so as to prevent, so far as is reasonably practicable, access to the guns by unauthorised persons'. This particular cabinet has bottom and top door locking and a small interior cupboard for ammunition. For purposes of illustration, a brick wall is shown behind: cabinets such as this must be rawl-bolted to a substantial, not stud-type, wall when in situ for real (courtesy of Raker Ltd).

storage requirements for air rifles, since February 2011, there has been a requirement under the Crime and Security Act 2010 that airgun owners must 'take reasonable precautions to stop unauthorized access to their airguns by people under the age of 18'.

Who can have an air rifle?
Provided that an air rifle has a muzzle energy of less than 12 foot pounds, no licence is required to buy, possess or use them. However, it is the owner/user's responsibility to ensure that the gun does not exceed these power levels as to do so would cause you to be guilty of being in possession of a firearm.

Age limits
Over the age of 18, anyone may buy an air rifle and ammunition and use them on private land where they have permission to shoot. Until recently, it was the case that, aged between 14–17, you could borrow and use an air rifle without supervision on land where you had permission to shoot and children under 14 could use such guns on private land (with permission) but only whilst under the supervision of an adult over the age of 21. The Crime and Security Act 2010 (which came into effect in February 2011) now means that, technically at least, anyone who allows a person under the age of 18 access to an airgun commits an offence.

Do I need a game licence?
First introduced in the 1800s as an enforcement tool against poaching, the game licence was pretty archaic and ineffectual so, in 2007, it was decided that one was unnecessary to shoot game in England and Wales. Scotland and Northern Ireland, however, did not follow suit until 2011.

Fox Control

Night-time lamping is, arguably, one of the most efficient ways of controlling foxes in a particular area. It does, however, have its opponents.

Lamping at night
Although there are no specific legal restrictions on the night shooting of foxes and any authorised person may carry out this form of fox control, it is essential to ensure that, both in the interests of safety and good neighbourliness, you comply with the guidance laid out in the BASC's Lamping Code of Practice. In addition, think of the following points:

• Familiarise yourself with all legal requirements, including always carrying your firearms or shotgun certificate, together with any written permission – and obviously only use the appropriate firearms and ammunition in accordance with the conditions of your firearms or shotgun certificate.

- Inform landowners, tenants and neighbours of your intentions and, where possible, give them a rough idea of the length of time you expect to be out.

- As a matter of courtesy, inform the local police who you are, and where you will be shooting.

- Shooting from any sort of vehicle is obviously potentially dangerous and so it is important that you take heed of the BASC advice that a safety procedure must be explicitly agreed with the driver and 'lamp-man' before shooting commences.

Using fox snares

It is important to remember that the United Kingdom is one of only five member states of the EU that permits the use of snares; the others being France, Belgium, Ireland and Spain.

Fox snares are a very effective means of fox control but it is essential that none is used carelessly or illegally. In the UK, as a result of the Wildlife and Countryside Act (section 6) there are legal restrictions on the kind of snares allowed to be used. These include:

- Not setting a snare in any place likely to catch a 'non-target species' such as roe deer, hares and badgers.

- Not using self-locking snares – free-running snares must have a permanent 'stop' fixed approximately 23cm from the eye of the snare.

In addition, the DEFRA Code of Practice on the Use of Snares in Fox Control reiterates that 'snares must only be set at sites likely to be used by foxes' and adds that 'snares should incorporate a strong swivel near the anchor point and also at a position closer to the noose. The wire must not be of less than 208kg breaking strain.' They also remind us that, by law, snares must be checked at least once a day – BASC recommendations go a step further and suggest that snares should be inspected twice daily (and as soon after dawn as is practicable).

Beware foreign imports

Be careful if you're tempted to buy fox wires on an internet trading site rather than through your usual game supplies retailer as some being imported (most commonly from China) could well be illegal. One snare in particular is labelled as being as being 'suitable for trapping rabbit, fox and small and medium-sized animals'. While some components may be lawful, other parts of the snare's make-up may not ... as a Scottish Gamekeepers Association (SGA) spokesman recently said, 'It is the trap operator that is legally responsible for its legality. Traps being sold from abroad, for example, may not meet UK standards.'

Cage traps for foxes work by having a bait at one end and a trap door at the other. As the fox enters and pulls at the bait (which is normally connected to the door via a rod), the door drops and the animal is caught (photo courtesy of Patrick Pinker game farms and equipment suppliers).

Do cage traps work?

'Catch-em alive' fox traps are used quite successfully by urban local authorities – but there, foxes are pretty well humanised by their daily living and are well used to things that a rural fox will find extremely alien.

Try one by all means, but my experience is that a cage trap (expensive to buy and difficult to transport on a regular basis) is not likely to encounter much success on the rural shoot.

Disguise it well, bait it with something attractive to a fox and you might just catch the odd, unsuspecting young cub – or, more controversially, a fox which has been 'dumped'.

Fox 'dumping' – fact or fiction?

Almost any gamekeeper will tell you of somewhere near them where urban foxes have been released by so-called 'do-gooders'. In 2003, the Union of Country Sports Workers looked into the subject of fox dumping in the countryside, but never published their findings. A press release by them published at the 2011 Game Fair said: 'We did a lot of work in 2003 … It appeared to be a nationwide problem and much, but by no means all of it, was anecdotal evidence.' It is their intention to re-open their research and they are hoping that '…this time we can really prove, once and for all, whether fox dumping in the countryside is fact or fiction'.

Understanding the Hunting Act 2004

In straightforward terms, the Hunting Act 2004 made it illegal to hunt a wild animal with dogs – unless that is, 'that hunting is exempt'. Which means what? Basically, that which is still permitted includes:

- stalking and flushing out mammals with no more than two dogs
- the use of a dog (terrier) below ground to protect game birds
- rat and rabbit hunting
- falconry
- rescue of a wild animal
- research and observation.

Of these various exemptions, it is likely to be the first three of these categories which will be of interest to you.

As regards the flushing of foxes from cover with no more than two dogs, the land must be either owned by those doing so, or be land on which the person has express permission from the owner.

Regarding the use of a dog below ground to protect game birds, the same applies – and you must not use more than one terrier at any one time. You must

For centuries, hunting has been a traditional country sport – and a pretty effective way of controlling foxes! The Hunting Act 2004 has changed all that and whilst it's still legal to hunt in certain circumstances, there are many restrictions to consider and rules to abide by.

also ensure that it is a fox earth and not a badger sett – if you or your terrier as much as puts a foot or paw near such a place, you might just find yourself charged with offences under the Protection of Badgers Act 1992 (see also below). Amongst other things, the current code of practice states that:

• The terrier's role must be to locate and bolt the fox in order that it can be shot.

• A 'hard' dog, likely to fight rather than bolt a fox, should not be used – whereas a 'soft' dog (known to habitually stand off and bark at the fox) should be.

• The terrier's time underground should be kept to the minimum and the dog must always be fitted with a locating device to its collar in order that its exact position underground can be monitored at all times.

Rat hunting with dogs is legal – as long as you have permission – as is rabbitting. Should you be using whippets, greyhounds, lurchers or any other type of 'running' dog, you must, however, be careful not to lay yourself open to the charge of hare-coursing, which is illegal under the Act.

It is also worth noting that the Hunting Act 2004 amended various other pieces of legislation so as to confer further protection to animals – these include the Protection of Animals Act 1911, Wild Mammals (Protection) Act 1996, Protection of Badgers Act 1992 and section 35 of the Game Act 1831.

Birds of Prey

Birds of prey (of any description) are protected! You can attempt to deter them, but there are no circumstances at all where you can kill them. Deterrents have included all manner of ingenious methods, including strips of silver foil and even CD discs left spinning on a thread in the hope that the sudden flash as the light catches them might cause them to fly off scared.

Flashing amber road-lights have been put to good use at night to protect newly released pheasants from being harassed by tawny owls in the release pen and there are advocates of leaving a radio tuned to a speaking station, in the hope that the sound of human voices might put off both birds of prey and foxes. In fact, it was only recently that I heard a report of a UK nature reserve that is now using radios tuned into BBC Radio 4 as a means of keeping foxes away from ground-nesting birds.

Identifying the presence of owls and sparrowhawks

Owl damage is easily recognised: only in the first few evenings after release are killed poults likely to be carried off and any dead birds found early in the morning with a crushed skull cannot really have been killed by anything other than an owl. Sparrowhawks are another thing entirely and unless you happen to disturb one on a kill, it can be several days before you realise that there are any in the area.

You might see feathers where a poult has been killed, but the most likely signs of a sparrowhawk come from watching the pheasants themselves. If they spend most of the time huddled under bramble and other release pen cover and seem afraid to venture out in search of food and amusement, then it is a pretty safe bet that there is a hawk somewhere in the neighbourhood.

Likewise, if you are hand feeding and birds on the ride suddenly panic and dash for cover if a blackbird sounds a warning or a harmless wood pigeon flies over, there is almost certainly a hawk working the woods on a regular basis.

Controlling Corvids

Larsen traps

Larsen traps are exceptionally effective in the spring when all types of corvids become extremely territorial and can be caught relatively easily.

A 'Larsen' is a legally permissible 'catch-em alive' cage trap. The attention of the would-be captee is drawn by a decoy bird which resides in a side compartment to the trap. Being tremendously territorial, the outside bird is all too keen to drop in to the trap and enter by perches set either by top or side doors. As the bird alights, its weight on the perch triggers a spring-loaded 'door'.

Where to place a Larsen trap

It might sound obvious to say that Larsen traps are best positioned where corvids are regularly seen, but be sure to place them within easy view of a look-out tree used by magpies and crows as they alight somewhere along a hedgerow or in the corner of a wood.

Despite seeing birds regularly in a particular area, your trap may, for some unknown reason, fail to catch – moving it just a few yards, or to the other side of the hedge, may be all that is required in order for it to become suddenly successful.

Taking care of the 'decoy'

There have been recent court cases built around the fact that some keepers have failed to provide 'adequate shelter and protection from adverse weather' to a decoy bird whilst contained within a Larsen trap. Make sure that you are not open to the same allegations should your trap be seen by a member of the public who may well then inform a local RSPCA inspector or similar.

What to feed the 'decoy'

The decoy bird will take everything it might find in its natural environment such as road-kill, naturally occurring carrion and eggs. For practical purposes, most keepers feed their decoys rabbit offal – heart, liver and lights – but don't bother with the intestines as they won't touch them. By far the easiest way of feeding the decoy bird is, however, to use tinned cat or dog food.

A Larsen trap is probably the most popular type of cage trap in which to catch magpies and crows...

...there are, however, other types such as this 'ladder' or 'letter-box' trap whereby bait is placed inside the trap and crows, jackdaws and rooks enter through the gaps in the top. Once they are in there, they are unable to fly out.

Shooting corvids

Exploit their natural tendencies and make a natural-looking nest of twisted grass or fine twigs placed out in the open about 25 metres away from a hide position in areas where corvids are known to frequent. In the nest, place a couple of hen's eggs (maybe even breaking one of the eggs to show off the yolk).

Whether shooting with an air rifle or a shotgun, you need to be well camouflaged; and that includes a hat, head-net and gloves to hide those tell-tale patches of exposed skin.

A plastic decoy owl might make magpies and crows want to mob it and, in doing so, come within shooting distance. Almost all shooting and agricultural supplies sell such things, but it is important to look at the eyes of the decoys before buying one! Only buy those with a definitive shiny yellow eye that contains a jet-black pupil – others, for some reason, just do not work half as effectively.

Stoats and Weasels

Whereas at one time, stoats and weasels used to be high on every gamekeeper's list of 'what I don't want to see on my shoot', times have changed. It was, admittedly, when a lot of shooting relied on wild, rather than reared birds (stoats can kill a sitting hen and both are quite partial to eggs and young chicks); even so, it is my personal experience that the numbers of stoats and weasels are far fewer than they once were.

However, should you have the time to run a 'trapping line' during the spring and early summer months (remember that, by law, such traps should be checked at least once every 24 hours), you will, undoubtedly, pick up several of either – for which not only will wild game be thankful, but so too will all manner of ground-nesting wild birds.

Making a 'tunnel' to house a trap

Most keepers use the Fenn Mk 4 Spring Trap, to accommodate which (and to remain within the law), you will need to build an artificial tunnel by scooping out a narrow, shallow trench just wide enough to accommodate the trap, placing some boards or bricks over the top and covering it with soil. An even simpler method is

A Fenn spring trap – in 'sprung' position and shown on concrete for illustrative purposes.

to nail three pieces of board together, or, depending where you are setting traps, make a tunnel from three breeze-blocks or several house bricks. You must, at each end, make sure that some method (stones, pegs of hazel, logs) restricts access to 'non-target' species.

Mink

In other countries, the European mink is protected by law. The 'wild' mink we have in the UK are, however, merely a feral off-shoot of the American mink which was introduced and farmed for its fur value. Not often would I ever advocate the total eradication of any animal or bird, but on this occasion, I think it important to stress the damage that feral mink do to the country's indigenous wildlife.

You should make every effort to kill them by whatever legal means are possible. In reality, this means either cage traps or 'spring traps' as defined by the Spring Traps Approval Order 1995; the latter of which include the Fenn Mk 5, the Payne Mk 1 and the Victor Conibear 120-2.

As far as 'catch 'em alive' cage traps are concerned, a rat trap or similar will just not do – the mesh is too thin and a mink will chew through it within minutes. A cage trap made expressly for mink is your only option. Once caught, the mink should be dispatched with a low-velocity air pistol or similar (see 'Who can have an air rifle?' earlier in this chapter). Do not ever be tempted into killing any targeted animal in a cage with a weapon more highly gauged as there is, by doing so, the very real danger of personal injury as a result of ricochet – and it won't do your trap any good either!

Do some good with what you're doing
Purely out of interest, as it is legally allowed to cull mink, you might like to help any local projects with your findings. The Berks, Bucks & Oxen Water Vole Recovery Project, for example, would, at the time of writing, love to hear from anyone 'trapping mink … or who could help with humane dispatch' in the interest of their research.

Rats

Rats have, over the years, given me some exciting sport with terriers and for those like me who have a fear of them, there is nothing more adrenalin and hair-sticking-up-on-the-back-of-your-neck inducing, than to be in a confined space when rats attempt to scramble up the wall and along the overhead beams of a barn whilst pursued by a small pack of motley terriers. Generally, however, the most efficient way of ridding a place of rats is by poison.

Poisoning

There are so many types on the market that it is difficult to know which to choose. Personally, I prefer to use either the waxed blocks or the sort that you lay as bait whilst still in a plastic sachet. Knowing the rat's propensity to chew anything plastic, the manufacturer's idea is that the poison will remain unaffected by damp and will stay fresh until it is gnawed upon. They can be tucked safely behind feed bins or placed in short lengths of drainpipe laid out specifically as baiting points.

Avoiding accidental death to livestock

Left in a quiet place, the rats will probably feel safe enough to eat the bait where they find it – but it is important that any other form of livestock does not have access to the immediate area just in case rats attempt to drag it away. The checking of these baiting points should become part of the daily routine – empty sachets being removed and replaced with new ones.

Preventing bait-shy rats

Whenever the subject of rat poison is discussed, there are always those who claim that rats have become immune to the anticoagulant type of poison such as Warfarin. One theory is that they have not in fact, become immune, more that some have survived ingesting small doses and as a consequence, become 'bait-shy'. It is for this reason that it is important to ensure that there is always a sufficient supply of poison once a baiting programme is begun. It will also pay you to periodically change the type of poison being used.

Trapping

Trapping, either by means of spring traps such as the Fenn Mk 4 or the old-fashioned 'catch 'em alive' wire trap, is effective.

Unlike the Fenn trap, a cage trap will require baiting. Ordinary poultry food will suffice but oatmeal, bacon fat or bananas (yes really!) all seem to attract rats. Surprisingly, the old traditional stand-by of cheese features very low down on the rat's list of favourite food.

Where rats are well established, it might seem a good idea to place the traps near to the burrow entrance but in practice, this only scares the old ones and it is better to trap away from the immediate vicinity of their home.

Keeping rats out of buildings

DEFRA reckon that the UK rat population is around the 60 million mark – that's a rat each for every man, woman and child should any of us wish for such a pet! Their increase is, according to the experts, due to milder winters (although the ones of 2009/10 and 2010/11 proved an exception to the rule!), which allow rats to breed all the year round and also to the fact that there is generally more edible rubbish being left around. Another reason sometimes given is that the water authorities are no longer as proactive as they once were, therefore the number of rats underground is escalating astonishingly.

As with most things, it is easier to prevent an invasion of rats onto your shoot and around your rearing houses and kennels than it is to eradicate them once they have set up home.

- Make every effort to prevent their access by laying down concrete floors.

- Place gratings on drains and small mesh wire over any openings.

- Rats will find it easier to enter a building if the walls are covered in ivy or similar vegetation and will use it as a ladder in order to enter a building from under the eaves.

Rats should be eradicated at every opportunity. On the shoot they will take food from around the hoppers and make burrows in and around partridge pens; around the rearing field and store rooms they can cause severe problems by chewing through cables, water piping, feed bags and, on occasions, killing young chicks – in addition to which, they are known carriers of disease (photo courtesy of Robert Stephenson).

Grey Squirrels

Game feeding sites encourage both rats and grey squirrels. Let alone the damage that grey squirrels do to trees, it is reckoned that they cost the British economy an estimated £14 million per annum – according to a study published jointly in 2011 by DEFRA, the Scottish Government and the Welsh Assembly. The report, by an international scientific organisation, found that greys harmed timber production and biodiversity, and damaged buildings. Reason enough to suggest that effective grey squirrel control is essential for not just shooting enthusiasts!

Should your land be known to be home to red squirrels (sadly, very rare in this day and age), you will not, by law, be able to either trap or poison grey squirrels for fear of catching or eradicating their smaller, far prettier and non-destructive cousins.

> **Squirrels carrying tree disease**
>
> Recent, but at the moment anecdotal, evidence suggests that trees damaged by grey squirrels are particularly prone to Phytophthora ramon infection which grey squirrels are carrying from tree to tree. George Farr, chairman of the European Squirrel Initiative, said, in the summer of 2011, that reports coming in from forestry workers 'reinforce the importance of the removal of grey squirrels and the devastating impact they are having on our woodlands and ecosystem'.

Trapping

For any shoot, plenty of tunnel traps are one of the best options – buy, or get the estate to buy, as many traps as can be a) afforded and b) checked on a daily basis. Legally, traps need to be set in positions where any 'non-target species' cannot gain access and so tunnel traps are the best solution.

Tunnel traps not only catch squirrels, they also have the potential to control many other pests around the feed rides, such as rats. (As an aside, poking out squirrel dreys in early spring is another control option and can provide some interesting and exciting shooting!)

Poisoning

Poisoning grey squirrels is no simple matter and, although it can be done, there are certain restrictions as to its use. It is, for example, only to be done for tree protection between 15 March and 15 August, using only approved hoppers.

Users must follow the guidelines issued by the Forestry Commission and detailed in their Practice Code Note 4, 'Controlling grey squirrel damage in woodland'. As mentioned above, it cannot be used under any circumstances where red squirrels (or pine martens) may be present. There is a wonderfully informative website of value to anyone with a need to control grey squirrels: www.greysquirrelcontrol.co.uk/poison.html

> ### Pest control in Northern Ireland
>
> In a slight diversion from predator control normally being the remit of gamekeepers, but one which could, nevertheless, be of interest to farmers in Northern Ireland who run a small shoot, they might like to learn of a pest control scheme in operation there.
>
> Organised jointly between BASC Northern Ireland and the Ulster Farmers' Union (UFU), the scheme is intended to put farmers who are in need of pest control in touch with people who shoot.
>
> BASC NI has recently set up a register of members and they hope that farmers experiencing pest and predator problems will contact them. BASC NI will then put UFU members in touch with their closest registered BASC members. A 'win-win' situation, I think!

The Spring Traps Approval Order 1995

In September 1995, The Spring Traps Approval Order listed the spring traps which could legally be used to kill certain mammals. This order related to England and Wales and revoked the previous legislation listed below:

The Spring Traps Approval Order 1975
The Spring Traps Approval (Variation) Order 1982
The Spring Traps Approval (Variation) Order 1988
The Spring Traps Approval (Variation) Order 1993

In addition there have been various amendments to the 1995 Order in 2007, 2009 and 2010 adding various new spring traps as they have been approved by DEFRA. Also, in October 2010, The Spring Traps Approval Order (Wales) listed the spring traps which could legally be used in Wales and revoked The Spring Traps Approval Order 1995 in so far as it applied to Wales.

In Scotland, on 19 August 1996, The Spring Traps Approval Order (Scotland) listed the spring traps which could legally be used in Scotland and revoked the following legislation:

The Spring Traps Approval (Scotland) Order 1975
The Spring Traps Approval (Scotland) (Variation) Order 1982
The Spring Traps Approval (Scotland) (Variation) Order 1988
The Spring Traps Approval (Scotland) (Variation) Order 1993

The 1996 legislation has not been varied since.

Ferreting

While not exactly 'predators', rabbits can, however, cause problems both on the shoot (damage to game crops and the like) and to farmers. As a gamekeeper you might, therefore, be asked to control rabbit numbers and, whilst there are numerous ways of doing so (shooting being an obvious one), ferreting rabbits into nets positioned carefully over the entrance and exit holes of a bury just has to be one of the most humane – as well as offering some exciting sport at the right time of the year.

If you've never kept ferrets before, it's probably best to find someone who has and pick their brains on the subject. In addition you should:

• Buy, or borrow some books on the subject – there are plenty around.

• Check out the UK webpages appertaining to ferreting, especially those of a club or association such as the Heart of England Ferret Association (email: info@hefa.org.uk)

• When the time comes, buy only animals from a known and reputable supplier and be very cautious about making a purchase from 'a man down the pub' or selling stock from the boot of his car at a country fair or similar.

Rabbit numbers around the estate (particularly around those all-important game crops) can often be controlled during the winter and early spring months by the use of ferrets. Not only is ferreting an efficient way of doing the job, it provides some exciting sport; it pays to handle your ferrets though – there's nothing more painful than a nip from an unfriendly one!

CHAPTER 5

Laying Pens and Breeding Stock

Although it seems that fewer shoots are rearing their own birds from stock caught up on the estate once the shooting season has finished, some are, and for that reason, it is very important to include this chapter. Also, whilst they might not bother with a laying pen, several do catch up a certain amount of hens and offer them to a local game farmer in return for chicks or six-week-old poults.

A Word of Caution

If it is necessary for whatever reason, to begin catching up as soon as shooting finishes, any freshly-caught or over-wintered hens should, perhaps, be kept in some sort of holding pen before being placed in the laying pens – especially if the weather is wet or there's chance of snow. Grass runs that become muddy in the early part of the year because of the constant traffic of birds' feet have little or no chance of recovering and they will either end up looking like a First World War battlefield or, when the weather does improve, a concrete carpark.

It is not a good idea to keep pheasants for too long in a covered building though, especially if artificial lighting is added to the equation. A few days or a couple of weeks should be okay, but if you leave them in there for too long, the birds will become less hardy and probably start laying before you want them to. Their laying potential will, in all probability, also be checked once the birds are eventually turned out into the large open-air runs.

Laying Pen Essentials

Traditional laying pens need to be as large as practicable for the amount of birds intended to be kept and they must be carefully situated. The pen should be well drained and surrounded by some form of windbreak. At one time, most keepers used corrugated tin sheeting which made a very efficient barrier, but this is nowadays quite an expensive option and it is far cheaper (and easier) to use a roll or two of windbreak material normally found in garden centres or surrounding tree nurseries.

If smaller pens made up of rearing sections are the preferred option, then the wind is not too great a problem as the baffle boards found on most pen sections will protect the inhabitants from the worst of any prevailing winds.

Where possible, the laying pen should be positioned in such a way that it catches the morning sun yet is protected from its hottest rays at lunchtime and in the early afternoon. At least part of the run should provide some shade at all times of the day.

What to add in the pen

Inside the laying pen itself, there should be fir boughs or similar, under which the hens can lay their eggs out of the wind and away from the unwanted attention of cock birds. Although many people use them in the laying pens, I am not an advocate of straw bales, but there is no doubt that they provide barriers behind which pheasants can shelter no matter from which direction the wind is blowing. Short-length barriers of corrugated sheets held up by stout posts and set at different angles dotted around the pen will have the same effect and, unlike straw bales, will not add to the possible risk of fungal disease.

A conventional laying pen complete with corrugated tin shelters for the birds as protection against the weather and also offering a secluded place in which the hens can lay their eggs. The provision of such shelter is, though, rather sparse in this particular instance and the runs could have perhaps benefited from the inclusion of a few fir boughs (photo courtesy of Philip Watts).

Raised Laying Units

In Britain, for possibly half a century or more, laying pairs of partridge (particularly grey partridge) have been kept for the duration of the breeding season in raised units. More recently, some game farms began using such units for pheasant breeding – each one holding a single male and several females – a situation that did not necessarily meet with the approval of everyone concerned with the world of shooting and animal welfare.

Some suggestions

Amongst suggested ways of 'enriching' a breeding pen are to provide laying pheasants and partridge with sufficient nesting areas for the numbers of birds. Where appropriate (partridges do not generally roost), there should also be suitable perches provided. In addition, the Game Farmers' Association (GFA) is of the opinion that the nesting areas are of great importance as they offer privacy to hens and, if well-designed 'can also provide surfaces for claw shortening and normal pecking behaviour. Nest boxes incorporating sand will enable dust-bathing and, where grit of the correct size is included, will meet another specific requirement of the code.'

> ### Don't fall foul of the law
>
> A report released in 2008 by the Farm Animal Welfare Council (FAWC) stated that if raised laying cages were to be considered, they should be 'enriched' rather than 'barren'. In 2010, the relevant government departments in England, Wales and Scotland used the FAWC's findings in order to come up with suitable Codes of Practice for those involved in game rearing. Effective since January 2011, anyone found not adhering to these codes might nowadays just be at risk of prosecution under the Animal Welfare Acts of 2006.

Flooring and roofing

The code also makes mention of the use of 'dry litter' and 'appropriate' flooring. Many raised units have weld-mesh floors and the use of Astroturf has been suggested as a possible floor covering. The GFA say that whilst this method will undoubtedly work, such flooring must be kept dry as, otherwise, droppings will clog and disease may occur. On the subject of flooring in units where the eggs roll to the outside once laid, the GFA say that the angle of the floor must not be too steep and that any materials used will 'have to take account of the need for eggs to roll out without getting caught up'.

Finally, on the subject of roof covering, the parts of the pen open to the elements must be covered by soft netting that will not damage the heads of birds should they be startled and jump up, and the roofed or solid-covered area should, to be in accordance with the code of practice, provide 'sufficient shelter for all birds'.

NB: As an interesting aside, the commercial poultry world were, in January 2012, compelled by EU legislation to keep their laying hens in colony or enhanced cages rather than in traditional battery units.

Freshly captured hens will soon adapt to the relative confines of the traditional laying pen (photo courtesy of Philip Watts).

Catching Up Breeding Stock

Ideally, there should be a couple of weeks between the end of the shooting season and commencing to catch up birds for the laying pen: this gives pheasants the chance to settle into some sort of feeding routine after the disturbances of the shooting days and to concentrate birds into a few specific areas (rather than having small pockets dotted throughout the estate).

It is important to set a day for catching (most often weather dependent) and to pick up as many birds as quietly and efficiently as possible. Pheasants and partridges will not tolerate being constantly frightened and, if not caught the first time, but, nonetheless, witness the panic of those which are being collected from the catchers, will be extremely wary of any future attempts.

Position the catchers a week or so before you need them and prop them up in such a way that birds can feed underneath and get used to them well before catching up commences.

How to catch them

Most people nowadays use up-turned pen sections fitted with funnels similar to those found around the bottom of a release pen and covered with soft netting which will prevent pheasants and partridges from damaging their heads. However, on the small shoot, there may still be a place for the old-fashioned hazel catchers, or for

A well-planned and perfectly located series of laying pens should look as good at the end of the rearing season as they did at the beginning. Here a sheltered spot keeps away the worst of the wind whilst still allowing plenty of sunshine. Before building a pen in such a place, it is as well to ensure that the area is not liable to flooding – choosing a location in the winter when things are at their wettest will help in avoiding such a scenario. Overhead nylon netting negates the need for brailles – see 'Some possible problems' below (photo courtesy of Alan Waugh/Stuart Fairhead/Heath Hatcheries).

smaller wire netting catchers which will hold half a dozen birds. One Surrey keeper I knew caught most of his hens whilst feeding and with only the aid of a landing net.

Some possible problems
Caught-up birds could have latent disease problems which may not be troublesome in the wild, but nevertheless might be encouraged to surface by the stress of catching up and subsequent confinement in the laying pen. However, with good management techniques the potential disease problems will be lessened or, most likely, fail to appear at all.

Feather-pecking and egg-eating
Because of being relatively closely confined, laying birds are potentially prone to feather-pecking and, more likely, egg-eating so some rearers fit their pheasants with 'specs' for the duration of the period they are in the pens. They should, though, perhaps be avoided wherever possible as recent research has suggested that even clip-on types (as opposed to those fitted with a pin through the bird's nostrils, which are frowned upon by the BASC and other game-rearing related organisations) can cause damage to the nasal septum and, theoretically at least, their use may therefore risk prosecution under the Animal Welfare Act 2006.

Bruised wings from brailles

With an open-topped communal laying pen, it is obviously necessary to decide on some way of preventing adult stock from flying out. Nets are generally impracticable in such situations and so this is most commonly done by clipping the primary feathers of one wing.

There are those, though, who prefer the use of brailles. Brailles, either cotton 'figure-of-eight' or 'strap' types, work by keeping one wing closed and, if fitted incorrectly, can cause the pheasant's wing to become bruised and damaged. It is, therefore, important to mention that great care must be taken when applying them and they must (perhaps obviously) be removed before releasing laying stock back onto the shoot. In fact, on balance, even though they are still currently legal to use, it is my considered, personal opinion that you should avoid situations where brailles might be necessary.

Just the Tonic

In 2012, Elanco launched a new game bird product that could prove just the tonic for gamekeepers (well, their laying birds and poults anyway!). Following on from the acquisition of Janssen Animal Health, Elanco extended the former company's existing 'tonic' range by including Game Bird Tonic HD Plus – which contains a vitamin D3 metabolite and a natural antioxidant blend; the idea being to support birds during the most demanding periods of spring-time laying.

Some medicinal details

The vitamin D3 metabolite has been shown to increase egg weights and improve feed conversion and feed intake. It is apparently more available to the body than vitamin D3, which plays a role in calcium metabolism (and therefore egg production). The benefits should be significant for commercial game farmers but also for the private shoot, as egg size correlates with chick weight. The metabolite can also improve bone strength, potentially resulting in healthier, more robust poults.

How vitamins are absorbed and used

The antioxidant blend incorporated into the tonic contains natural preparations of vitamins that are better absorbed and used in the body, as well as more complex antioxidants found in fruits and vegetables, such as flavanoids, polyphenols and carotenoids. Antioxidants

A proprietary game bird 'tonic' might just help increase fertility, egg-laying and subsequent hatchability – at least according to scientific research carried out on behalf of the manufacturers (photo courtesy of Elanco Ltd).

mop up free radicals produced by day-to-day metabolism, which would otherwise cause cell damage or play active roles in the development of some diseases. The requirement for antioxidants can be increased in certain physiologically stressful situations – such as when additional demands are placed on the body by production. So now you know!

Breed from Only Legally Allowed Stock

Over the years there have been new imports of pheasants – most recently the Kansas – but, in the quest for a bird that flies well and holds its ground, many others have been tried and crossed. In the words of one modern-day game farmer:

Just about every species and sub-species has been crossed by now. Everyone's still trying to improve flying and holding qualities. Sometimes they get it wrong and the birds are too wild and stray off ... Japanese greens are nice but they are not that fertile and don't produce as many eggs. The Michigans are good on fertility and rearing but exceptionally wild ... and there are dozens of crosses in between.

Legally, it is not possible to release just any kind of game bird into the wild and whilst an English ringneck pheasant, for example, is certainly okay to rear and release without breaking any laws, to do the same with an ornamental breed, a Lady Amherst, for instance, could possibly leave you open to prosecution under the Wildlife and Countryside Act 1981 – which makes it illegal to 'release into the wild any kind of animal or bird not ordinarily resident in, or not a regular visitor to Great Britain in a wild state'.

An example scenario

Keepers and game farmers had long been cross-breeding the Japanese pheasant with 'ordinary' pheasant varieties to improve the latter's flying ability – a combination of genetics which seemed to work well. When the Wildlife and Countryside Act was first introduced, there was much discussion as to whether or not the Japanese was an 'exotic' import as, if so, neither it nor its cross-bred offspring could be released onto British sporting estates. Eventually it was proven that having been introduced into the country during the Victorian period, it was theoretically possible that the make-up of every wild pheasant might already contain Japanese genes and the breed should therefore be considered to be indigenous!

Changing Bloodlines

Some estates periodically change the types of pheasants bred and released: most usually in the hope that doing so will increase the vigour and flying abilities of future generations (see also below). Whilst a certain breed or type might work well on one particular shoot, it does not necessarily follow that it will be suitable on your ground and so give all aspects careful consideration before contemplating a change.

Once you have – and if you are still of the opinion that a change is worthwhile – it makes sense in the first year to replace only half of your total number with new blood and to keep the other half as your normal strain. Wing-tagging the two lots with different coloured tags will enable you to see whether more or fewer birds of either group are shot during the forthcoming season – and therefore whether it is worthwhile converting fully to the new strain or carrying on with original stock and bloodlines.

Is Swapping Cocks Worthwhile?

For many years it has been traditional for keepers and others involved in game rearing to swap cock pheasants caught up on their estate with those caught up from one a fair distance away – the reasons given being that it would help prevent their resident stock from becoming 'in-bred'. Bearing in mind that one is likely to be using perhaps ten cock birds to 100 hens, the coefficient of inbreeding will be very low and it will be many years, if ever, before it becomes a serious problem.

More important to my mind is the fact that if one continually breeds from stock which has been caught up on any estate at the end of the season, you are likely to be using birds that have avoided being shot by dint of the fact that they were poor fliers. You are, therefore, potentially breeding a subsequent generation that will be even less likely to provide a sporting shot and it is at this point where many people consider the inclusion of other pheasant strains in order to bring in renewed vigour.

Potential Causes of Infertility

Whilst a percentage of infertile game eggs is inevitable, an unusual amount suggests that there is a problem in the breeding stock and/or its management.

Possible causes might be breeding from stock that are either too old, too young, were themselves badly hatched and reared, or which have suffered from health and disease issues. Other reasons might include poor laying pen conditions, a bad diet, disturbed mating – or preferential mating whereby, for some unknown reason, a cock bird will mate with some hens but not others – the wrong ratio of cocks to hens, or apparent infertility which is in fact due to poor egg storage.

All seemingly infertile eggs left in the incubator after a hatch should therefore be opened and the yolk inspected for any signs of development: if any can be seen, then the egg was obviously fertile and the problem lies elsewhere.

CHAPTER 6

Incubation and Rearing

Most keepers set eggs regularly on a particular day of the week that suits them best, and from setting to hatching will take 24 days. The larger models of incubators are computer controlled, ensuring a consistent temperature and humidity throughout the process. They also turn the eggs automatically – sometimes as often as once every hour. Each model of incubator is, however, different and it is essential to follow the manufacturer's handbook rather than these rather general guidelines.

Incubators come in all shapes and sizes but are basically either forced-air or still-air. In the latter type, eggs remain in the incubator for the full duration, but when eggs are being incubated in forced-air types, they are, after 20 days, transferred to hatchers for the remaining period. These hatchers have an increased moisture content, enabling the chicks to break though their shell with greater ease and helping to ensure a more vigorous day-old chick.

What's the difference between forced-air and still-air incubators?

The difference is simply a fan. In forced-air incubators, a fan circulates the air around the incubator, keeping the temperature constant in all parts. The temperature can be measured anywhere within the airflow. In a still-air incubator, there is no fan, the heat stratifies (forms layers) inside the incubator so the temperature is different between the top and bottom of the incubator.

Where to House Your Incubator

Just any old shed or outhouse will not do and it is important to take note of the following points.

• Don't place the incubator in a small room or outhouse without ventilation or which is subject to variations in temperature.

• Don't place the incubator near the door, against the wall or in front of the window

Large shooting estates and professional game farmers house their incubators/setters in specially constructed and insulated rooms that can be easily cleaned and disinfected. Here such a room houses a Petersime setter: note the fact that egg trays are on a wheeled frame for easy management (photo courtesy of Alan Waugh/Stuart Fairhead/Heath Hatcheries).

– or anywhere where it will be subject to extremes of temperature.

• An incubator room should be between 18.3–21°C (64.94–69.8°F). Keep a max/min thermometer in the room at incubator level and record the temperature once a day.

Setting Your Eggs

Eggs have to be washed and disinfected before being graded and set in the incubators. Correct and safe solutions can be bought from your game equipment suppliers. Once eggs have been trayed up, they should ideally be kept in the same room as the incubators for around 12 hours before being set.

When setting eggs in tray inserts – the usual way with forced-air incubators – they should be placed either with the large end up, or horizontally with the large end slightly elevated. This enables the embryo to remain oriented in a proper position for hatching. Never set eggs with the small end upward.

Although more usual to lay setting eggs on their side in a still-air incubator, it is nowadays possible to buy plastic inserts which can be cut to fit the size of your incubator trays; this enables eggs to be placed in the same manner as that described above.

Plastic inserts make the setting of game bird eggs that much easier and safer. Note the different colours: the green being used to house regular-sized eggs and the white for those that are slightly larger (photo courtesy of Philip Watts).

Incubation

Poor hatching results occur most often because of incorrect temperature control and/or humidity, both of which interfere with the normal growth and development of the embryo. In addition, poor results can occur because of improper ventilation, egg turning and sanitation of the machines or eggs.

Obtain the best possible hatch by keeping the temperature at 37.7°C (100°F) throughout the entire incubation period when using a forced-air incubator. Very minor fluctuations can be tolerated without mishap but prolonged periods of high or low temperatures will undoubtedly alter your hatching success.

Still-air incubators should be kept at a marginally higher temperature of 38.8°C (102°F). Make sure of obtaining the correct temperature reading by having the bulb of the thermometer at the same height as the top of the eggs when the eggs are lying horizontally. If the eggs are positioned in a vertical position, raise the thermometer bulb to a point just below the top of the egg, but in either situation don't allow the thermometer's bulb to touch the eggs or incubator as if you do, incorrect readings will most likely result.

Egg turning
Most modern incubators have automatic turning facilities but just in case yours is

one of the ones that doesn't, the following observations may be of value. Eggs must be turned at least four to six times daily during the incubation period, but don't turn them at all during the last three days before hatching in a still-air incubator or after they've been moved from a forced-air one into the hatchers.

In a small still-air incubator, where the eggs are turned by hand, it may be helpful to place an 'X' on one side of each egg and an 'O' on the other side, using a pencil. This serves as an aid to determine whether all eggs are turned.

When turning by hand, be sure that your hands are free of all greasy or dusty substances as eggs thus contaminated may well suffer from reduced hatchability. In addition, take note of the fact that embryos have delicate blood vessels which rupture easily when severely jarred or shaken and too rough a treatment might well kill the developing chick.

Humidity and ventilation

Humidity must be carefully controlled in order to prevent unnecessary loss of moisture within the egg. The relative humidity in the incubator between setting and four days prior to hatching should remain at 55–60 percent and then be increased to 65 percent relative humidity for the final days.

Rarely is the humidity too high in properly ventilated still-air incubators. The water pan area should be equivalent to one-half the floor surface area or more. Increased ventilation during the last few days of incubation and hatching may necessitate the addition of another water tray or even something as simple as a wet sponge.

Some chicks may hatch out earlier than the rest (usually as a result of fresher eggs being set). You must not, however, be tempted into taking them from the incubator until the main hatch is complete as, once the door or lid is opened, vital humidity is lost – considerably reducing the chances of the rest of the eggs hatching out without mishap.

Ventilation

Ventilation is extremely important throughout the whole incubation process. While the embryo is developing, oxygen enters the egg through the shell and carbon dioxide escapes in the same way. As embryos grow, the air vent openings are gradually opened to satisfy increased embryonic oxygen demand. When chicks hatch, they require an increased supply of fresh oxygen and so care must be taken to maintain humidity during the hatching period. Unobstructed ventilation holes, both above and below the eggs, are essential for proper air exchange.

It is important not to attempt adding a new batch of eggs to ones that have been in the incubator for a while because, as we have seen, immediately prior to hatching game bird eggs require extra humidity, adversely affecting the other, younger eggs.

Cleanliness in the incubator

It is essential that the incubator is scrupulously cleaned and disinfected between each batch – your local game equipment supplier or local agricultural merchant can advise on the best solutions to use. The amount of chick down given off during hatching will block the shell pores of subsequent eggs and any harmful bacteria present will be able to multiply unhindered with a detrimental knock-on effect of reducing the hatchability of each successive hatch.

Cruel to be kind

There will always be a few eggs that chip, but do not hatch with the rest. Tempting though it is to help those still struggling from their shells, they will, unfortunately, never make good birds due to the fact that they have already been weakened. Also, deformed chicks sometimes hatch and it's not unusual to find a bird with an extra beak, a roach back or a wry neck as an unfortunate result of 'operator failure' – quite often the wrong degree of humidity. Kill them quickly and humanely by pressing their necks with your thumb over the edge of a table, dislocating the neck vertebrae.

Just as soon as a hatch has been completed, all the shells and debris should be cleaned out and disposed of safely…

…once all the eggs have been cleared and the chicks moved safely to the rearing units, everywhere must be cleaned and disinfected. NB: A face mask prevents the keeper from inhaling the fine dust given off by the chicks' downy covering (both photos courtesy of Philip Watts).

Rearing Fields

Although it is possible to rear game birds intensively, you cannot, in my opinion, beat rearing them on grass and that is not always possible to do if you are restricted by the immovability of a permanent building.

Of course, the more birds the estate rears, the more the problems associated with a permanent rearing field are likely to occur. At least with movable rearing sheds heated by calor gas and each containing between 200–300 poults, it should be possible to move houses, night shelters and runs onto some fresh ground from year to year – even if the actual rearing field itself remains the same.

On the rearing field it is important to maintain high standards of cleansing and disinfection to prevent the spread of disease between groups of birds. Remember too that many diseases are potentially present in a game bird's body but will not show signs until that bird is stressed – so be extra vigilant when bitting chicks or moving poults to the woods. At all times birds should have ready access to a high quality feed of a type appropriate to their age and any changes in ration should take place gradually.

NB: Contrary to what one might think, it is interesting to note that the first case of outbreak in a new rearing area or release pen is usually the worst. The reason is that the first birds raised on fresh ground have little exposure to infective oocysts – when they eventually become exposed, they have little or no immunity and the outbreak is particularly serious.

The benefits of grass

Grass keeps young chicks amused by pecking at it and also any insects it might harbour. The dew gives birds a little dampening off as they run through it after being let out first thing in the morning – and this in turn helps the feathers' natural protective body oils to develop. It is important, however, that the grass is not allowed to become long and straggly, as it could then do more harm than good by providing a home for fungal diseases such as aspergillosis. (For more on this, see Chapter 9 'Disease and Medication').

Avoiding grass-borne fungal diseases

To prevent such possibilities, mow the field before constructing the pens and then, if necessary, take a robust lawn mower or strimmer in there shortly before the chicks are due to arrive in order to cut a narrow 'pathway' all around the perimeter, diagonally from corner to corner and then finally, a central one from the pop-hole entrance of the night shelter. By doing so, young birds are more likely to find their way back to the source of heat, will be less inclined to congregate in pen section corners and will undoubtedly be easier to shut in at night.

Some Thoughts on Rearing Shed Sizes

Big isn't necessarily beautiful – or more successful; it is, in this instance though, possibly less time consuming. I have, in my time, tried rearing pheasant chicks in large sheds, each capable of holding 1,000 birds or more, but I remain convinced that, despite the undoubted extra work involved, you cannot beat the traditional rearing sheds with a night shelter and netted run attached.

In praise of small units

Small units lessen the chance of disease spreading quite so rapidly and also give the birds more opportunity to find space around the feeders and drinkers. Feather pecking might be a problem in a certain unit, but will only affect 200–300 birds rather than a shedful of 1,000 or more.

It is a strange fact that, despite there being no obvious difference between them, one small rearing unit might do worse than the one next door. Although problematic in itself, at least it is only a few birds affected rather than a good portion of this year's young stock, as may possibly be the case when rearing in large buildings.

The benefit of large buildings

On the other hand, big sheds are easier to clean, disinfect and fumigate and it's possible to get into every nook and cranny with the aid of a steam cleaner. Small plywood sheds, by contrast, do undoubtedly have a lot of inaccessible corners which could provide a home for undesirable parasites; unless, that is, you are prepared to dismantle them every autumn and clean every side, floor and roof before then re-building them at the beginning of the next rearing season.

A personal choice

Even accepting that they are more time consuming on a day-to-day basis, I would, however, much prefer the option of several small units rather than one big one and were I to be involved in a small DIY shoot where only a few hundred poults are to be released, would have absolutely no hesitation in opting to buy a couple of traditional sheds, night shelters and pen sections – even though it might initially be a more expensive option than merely sectioning off a portion of an available farm building.

How to Rear Your Chicks

Game bird chicks are notorious for their ability to die at the drop of a hat! If they can drown in a drinker, suffocate themselves in a corner of the brooder shed, or, at a later stage, become chilled in overlong wet grass out in the run, they will. It

---

Take sensible biosecurity precautions

- Place disinfectant footbaths at all main entrances to the rearing shed and/or field and change them regularly.

- Clean, disinfect and dry out housing and all related equipment between batches of birds.

- Ensure housing is always kept in good condition, clean and at an appropriate steady temperature, especially during the first three weeks.

- Make sure that pens are large enough to prevent overcrowding – a factor that can easily lead to stress in gamebirds.

- See that clean water is always available and the area surrounding drinkers is clean and dry.

- Likewise, keep feeders full and on dry ground so that they are less likely to become contaminated.

- Control access by wild birds and pests – many of which are well-known carriers of disease.

A beautifully constructed rearing field showing housing units, night shelters and, in this case, the grass runs are of the 'A' frame apex type rather than as is sometimes used, square runs made up of sections over which a nylon net is added. To prevent gas bottles running out and chicks becoming chilled, it might be worth considering equipping each house with two gas bottles and an automatic change-over system (photo courtesy of Alan Waugh/Stuart Fairhead/Heath Hatcheries).

is, therefore, important to think ahead and do all you can to alleviate any potentially disastrous situations.

If hatching and rearing for the first time, it will most definitely pay to go and pick the brains of an experienced gamekeeper or game farmer – most of whom will be happy to help and give you the benefit of their experience ... it is, after all, far better to learn from other people's mistakes than your own.

Artificial brooders

It makes sense to buy a brooder from the same place as you buy your incubator. There are many variations on the market, but the purpose of all of them is exactly the same: namely, to keep your day-olds warm! As with the incubator, it is important to carry out the maker's instructions to the letter. Temperature regulation is critical and birds should not be chilled at any time.

Most varieties of poultry brooders are suitable for rearing pheasant chicks, but one of the most effective is a calor-gas type. If considering using electricity, one of the simplest ways of providing heat is to use an infra-red heater suspended over an enclosed area. (The heater can be equipped with either a dull-emitter or a special bulb – the latter is, I think, best as it gives off a warm cosy glow which seems to encourage chicks to stay in its light.)

Pre-preparation

Because pheasant chicks are prone to getting into the corners of a brooder house, getting chilled and smothering one another, whatever heat source you use should be surrounded by a hardboard circle for the first few days.

Turn the brooder on, the day, or preferably, 24 hours before the chicks are due, in order that the immediate area will have thoroughly aired and there will be some ambient warmth – remember that your chicks will have just come out of an incubator with a running temperature of around 37.7–38.8°C (100–102°F). Make subsequent preparations depending on the type of brooder you have: with the hanging infra-red variety, for instance, it should be suspended about 45cm above the floor. When the chicks are introduced, allow about half an hour before you decide whether or not the heat source requires adjusting: if they are too cold, the chicks will be noticed standing on tip-toe in the centre and cheeping very loudly; if too hot, they will settle in a large ring around the sides. If, however, they spread comfortably under the heat source leaving a small clear area in the very centre, conditions are perfect.

'Hardening-off'

At some stage, you need to begin 'hardening-off' your poults and acclimatising them to being without heat. The makers of a specific brooding unit will, in the

Pheasant chicks under a calor gas brooder. Note the chick box lid being used as temporary (and easily disposable) crumb feed containers and the triangles of plywood fitted to the corner of the shed in order to stop birds crowding in the corners where they might suffocate one another (photo courtesy of Alan Waugh/Stuart Fairhead/Heath Hatcheries).

instructions which accompany their product, give advice as to weaning your chicks. Generally though, you should have been gradually raising the heat source a little each week so that, from an initial temperature of about 32°C (90°F), by the end of the third week the temperature is down to around 21°C (70°F) and may, on warm days, be switched off altogether. In any event, and in all but exceptionally bad weather, your birds should be totally off heat by the age of about four and a half weeks. If birds are being allowed access to the night shelters and run then this should be a gradual process and take into consideration the weather conditions.

Night shelters and outdoor runs
Although chicks are kept in the brooder house for the first few days of life, they need to be gradually exposed to the outside elements and this should be done by first affixing some sort of night shelter to the shed. Traditionally made to connect with the smaller types of brooder house, they are built of tanalised timber and covered on at least the roof and back by clear monoflex. The front incorporates a gate and the two ends a pophole each.

Sections (3m x 1.5m) for making outdoor runs are usually constructed of the same sort of timber with two 150mm boards at the base and are covered by 25mm mesh galvanised wire. They are available to purchase as either plain, gated or popholed. The tops of such runs will, of course, need to be covered with a canopy of soft nylon netting to prevent birds from escaping: the type of netting is important if you are to avoid pheasants flying up and injuring themselves.

Night shelters and sections ready to be placed onto fresh grass in preparation for a new rearing season (photo courtesy of Philip Watts).

Fitting Bits

The fewer birds each brooder shed and run contains, the less likelihood there is of problems with disease (see Chapter 9) or feather-pecking. However, practicalities and economics dictate differently and so in order to combat the latter problem, most keepers and game farmers fit bits to their birds at between two and three weeks of age. These prevent birds from fully closing their beaks and therefore grasping and pulling feathers from another bird.

Bits are available in three sizes: 'A', 'B' and 'C'. The first are for use on

Pushing poults into the night shelters from the outdoor runs prior to commencing bitting. The night shelter is the best place for such work as it confines the birds and allows a reasonable flow of fresh air.

A 'Bitfitter' complete with bit ready to go.

Bit fitted between the upper and lower mandible and held in place by being clipped into the nostrils. The pheasant poult here is of the melanistic type – hence the unusual feather colouring (all three photos in this sequence courtesy of Philip Watts).

partridges or pheasants between one and four weeks and the latter are intended for adult (breeding or over-wintered birds), so it is size 'B' that should be used at this stage. Nowadays most people use 'Bitfitter' bits because they are quicker and easier to apply with the use of a 'Bitfitter' tool; nevertheless, bags of loose bits are available and, with a little practice, can easily be fitted by hand. Whatever system is used, great care must be taken not to damage the top mandible of the poult.

It is important to remember that bits must be removed when the poults are taken from the rearing field to the release pens.

Hatching and Rearing with Broody Hens

While it's not quite modern twenty-first-century gamekeeping, there may still be the small shoot or interested amateur who wishes to use a broody hen to hatch and look after a few pheasants. Broodies are also useful in a situation where you might want to rear and release a clutch or two of grey partridge in the hope that they will eventually successfully colonise and create a nucleus of wild breeding pairs for the future.

A broody will save you the bother of worrying about humidity, air-flow and regular turning of the eggs. She is also unlikely to succumb to an electrical power failure but, despite that, no broody can be guaranteed to sit on her eggs for the full duration – which can be very disheartening and sad if she packs it all in with only a few days left before the chicks are due to hatch. However, should you wish to have a go, here are a few pointers which might lead to success.

• She will need a quiet secluded place in which to sit on her eggs: if at all possible, a small coop and run set well away from any distractions. If not, it will have to be a broody box in a suitable corner of a vermin-proof garden shed, garage or out-building. (It must not, however, be subject to fluctuations of temperature.)

• A nest can be made by means of first of all placing an upturned grass sod cut to the correct dimensions in the base of the broody coop or box and a saucer-like depression shaped in its centre (which will help retain necessary humidity). Next bank up the nest and sides of the box with suitable material – this would, at one time, invariably have been straw or hay, but there are nowadays, cleaner, more hygienic alternatives to be had – making sure that the corners are packed tightly and there is no way that eggs can roll out of the nest.

• Once you are absolutely certain that your chosen hen is broody, place a couple of dummy-eggs in the nest and then, in the evening, gently move her onto them and give her the following 24 hours to settle before very quietly and gently taking away the dummy eggs and replacing them with your precious game bird eggs.

• Depending on the hen (some take their duties so seriously, they will not leave the nest of their own volition), you can choose to either keep the box closed and remove her morning and early evening in order that she can feed, drink and empty herself, or place a supply of food and water in front of the box and leave her to her own devices. If you choose the former option, use great care when lifting her off the nest that she does not have any of the eggs caught in her feathers, otherwise they may fall and break as you bring her out.

• As incubation progresses, you will notice that she loses some of her breast feathers; this is quite normal and the area is known as the 'brood spot' – its purpose being to ensure that the bird's body heat is efficiently and correctly transferred to the eggs.

• A couple of days before the chicks are due to hatch, she will hear them cheeping and be very reluctant to leave the nest for either food or water. Even if you lift her out, she will, in all probability, be anxious to return to the box rather than feed or drink. A little water (at room temperature) mist-sprayed on the eggs and nest at this time will help in ensuring that there is sufficient humidity and that the shell membrane is not too dry.

• Once the majority has hatched, the broody hen will be quite happy to squat with her chicks in the same position as she's been in during incubation for perhaps as long as a day before she begins encouraging them to feed and explore. There is no need to worry about the youngsters not feeding during these first few hours because they will be getting enough sustenance from the yolk sac they absorbed immediately prior to hatching.

• The hen will look after her brood very well from now on – all you need to do is supply a safe environment free from vermin and disturbance, some food and water and let her do the rest.

A silkie bantam or silkie-cross type usually makes for a good broody and mother when one is hatching by old-fashioned methods. Although natural hatching is not very practical when it comes to rearing large numbers of birds, it might still have a place when only a few birds are being released or when a clutch or two of partridges are being put down onto the estate in order to add a bit of interest and excitement on a shooting day (photo courtesy of Robert Stephenson).

CHAPTER 7

Releasing Techniques

You cannot simply take young birds to a suitable part of the estate and release them straight into the wild. Both pheasant and partridge need a period of acclimatisation – which is best achieved by the use of large release pens for pheasants and smaller ones, usually made up of rearing sections, for partridges.

Releasing Partridges

Temporary sectional pens intended for the release of partridges should always be built big enough to comfortably house their occupants. Environment-wise (see 'Size matters' below), it is not so important because partridges will most likely be released from pens situated on stubble or in the corners of game crops which will be ploughed at a later date, but in an effort to prevent disease, it is crucial.

How to release partridge
Whilst the principles of partridge releasing have not changed in a big way over the last decade (see below), I think it is fair to say that modern thinking is that only red-legs, or French partridge, should be released on a seasonal basis when intended just for shooting. In fact, from talking to Mike Swan at the GWCT, it seems that they would actually 'discourage the releasing of greys on a seasonal basis just for shooting'. The thinking behind this statement is based on their recent research on the best methods for rearing and release of greys for re-establishment of wild populations. This clearly shows that ordinary brooder hut greys released as coveys have very poor survival and invariably fail to breed. Because of this they could easily cause damage to existing wild stocks.

These days fewer people release covey-sized groups of red-legs any more. Most concentrate on bigger pens and bigger groups, but the principles are much the same. Please note that the Code of Good Shooting Practice says birds should be out before the start of the shooting season, there should be no topping up, and that all temporary partridge pens are dismantled and taken away just as soon as all the partridges have been released. In addition, pens should be sited in cover crops, or other non-sensitive habitats, rather than on downland slopes, for example.

Partridges in a section pen prior to being trickle-released into a game crop mix of maize and sorghum (photo courtesy of Richard Barnes/Kings Game Cover).

Making a temporary release pen

The standard pen consists of several rearing pen sections made of chicken wire and covered with a net. Each section should have a board approximately 33cm wide along the bottom. Make sure that there are no holes and gaps. Any projection (nails, loose wire) must be removed to avoid damaging the birds.

Pen sections should be placed onto a 30cm-wide membrane strip (e.g. damp-proof membrane) to help prevent the birds digging around the edge of the pen.

Each bird must have sufficient access to food, clean water, grit and shelter from wind and rain at all times – pens should, therefore, also include brashings (deciduous and conifer) and/or a more substantial shelter in the form of a raised board or sheet of corrugated tin. An electric fence around the pen(s) will help to prevent predation by foxes and tunnel traps could be sited around the pen to keep rats, stoats and weasels at bay.

Finally, it is important to use the same type of feeders as the partridge have become used to during the weeks prior to release.

Releasing methods

You can release partridges from the pen a few at a time. Ideally, it should be done quietly over a period of days and via a pophole or small gate through which birds can wander at their discretion. In order to create the least disturbance possible, it might be an idea to rig up some sort of system whereby the pophole or whatever can be opened and dropped shut from a distance. Those released will then be encouraged to stay around the area by the calling of the birds that remain in the pen. However you choose to do it, it is important to adhere to the Code of Good Shooting Practice, the relevant part of which can be found on the British Association for Shooting and Conservation's website page: http://www.basc.org.uk//en/codes-of-practice/code-of-good-shooting-practice.cfm

---

Beware of over-stocking in sensitive areas

There have been recent cases whereby shoots have been taken to court as a result of over-stocking birds (generally pheasants) on particularly environmentally sensitive areas such as Sites of Special Scientific Interest (SSSIs). These have usually involved the building of release pens. There have, though, also been cases involving situations where game has been encouraged to feed in such places and too great a concentration has, in the eyes of the prosecutors, caused damage to the land and flora.

Constructing Pheasant Release Pens

The interior of any pheasant release pens should contain a mixed selection of trees and shrubs, sheltered areas and grassy sunning spots. They should also be large enough to contain the numbers of pheasants intended to be released there, but I'm sorry to say that, from my experience, they seldom are.

Size matters
A release pen will always benefit from covering as much area as possible. A pen adequate to happily contain a 1,000 birds or more is a huge undertaking and very expensive to build if it is constructed to ideal measurements.

To ensure pheasant release pens are not over-stocked (and therefore overcrowded), you should take the trouble to look at the Game and Wildlife Conservation Trust's 'Guidelines for Sustainable Gamebird Releasing'. In most circumstances, this indicates a stocking density of no more than 1,000 poults per hectare of pen, but is reduced to 700 birds per hectare for Ancient Semi Natural Woodland. (Try to avoid using ASNW and other potentially sensitive sites if you possibly can.)

It is amazing how quickly pheasant poults can strip a pen of vegetation – one minute you're looking at it thinking that your newly released birds will get lost in amongst it all and the next you can, when down on hands and knees, see from one end to the other. In most instances, the undergrowth will recover, but not if you use the same pen year in year out, in which case, the land will never recuperate.

Although not recently built, so much can be seen in this photo with regards to pen construction: plentiful cover – even at the end of the shooting season; a sunny, yet sheltered aspect; the use of small mesh netting and adequate straining wire; 'floppy' wire so as to make it difficult for predators to climb; two strands of electric fencing wire positioned around the base so as to prevent digging by foxes, badgers and dogs.

How to build a pen

Although initially expensive, a properly constructed release pen will last up to 20 years. It needs to be 2m in height. The perimeter is usually made up of two rolls of small-mesh wire netting: 3.2cm for the bottom half and 5cm for the upper half. The bottom 30cm is turned out and pegged down or buried, while the top 46cm is allowed to flop outwards in order to prevent predators from gaining access.

- Start by hammering in all the posts, which must be no more than four paces apart and sunk around 60cm into the ground.

- Struts angled at around 30 to 40 degrees to take the tension of the straining wire should be fixed to the corner posts and gateposts. Some people prefer to support their corner posts by means of wire windlasses pegged outside the fence line, like guy ropes on a tent. This is a particularly useful technique where the ground is rocky or hard.

• Next, attach the top straining wire as tightly as possible before doing the same with the middle wire, onto which the top and bottom rolls of wire netting will be fixed by either thin garden wire or fencing clips. Remember to allow a gap for a gate when fixing the middle wire.

• Staple the wire netting to the top of each post and tread it into a previously dug trench or bend it outwards if it is to be pegged.

• Backfill or peg before attaching the top roll of wire netting and then connect both to the middle straining wire.

• Pull the top of the roll upwards and clip or wire it to the top straining wire. It should then be possible to staple both rolls down each post, taking extra care around the gate.

• Around the whole of the perimeter, fix one or two strands of electric fencing to prevent foxes from coming too close. The fence should be about 45cm away from the perimeter and the first strand roughly 15cm above the ground; the second (if used), about the same height again above the first.

One or two strands of electric fence fixed around the perimeter of the release pen will help prevent foxes from digging in and stray dogs from coming too close.

Including anti-fox grids

Foxes remain the same size, so there's nothing much changed in the construction and fitting of anti-fox grids at strategic points around the release pen perimeter! The distance between the bars should be 9cm. The odd cub or small vixen may still squeeze through at this measurement, but anything narrower restricts access by the poults. For this reason, don't forget the addition of an electric fence as mentioned above. There is a fact sheet on release pen construction on the Game and Wildlife Conservation Trust's website: www.gwct.org.uk

A word about temporary pens

At one time, release pens were not the well constructed edifices they are now and were often nothing more than a few rolls of six-foot wire netting run round a clump of trees, pegged at the bottom and protected from foxes by the addition of an electric wire. They were quite often used as a means of holding small quantities of birds reared under broody hens and so didn't need to be very big. They were also almost always taken down and moved from year to year.

Such a system was used at my first employment as an under-keeper and it was my job to erect, dismantle and re-erect elsewhere in the same wood during the following spring – by which time there was little or no evidence of a pen ever having been there the previous summer. It is a system well worth still considering today, especially on the smaller DIY shoot.

An anti-fox grid – not in situ, but simply to show what one is!

Repairing and Improving Existing Pens

'Better the day, better the deed', is the old expression and it is one to be considered when contemplating work and improvements to existing release pens – it is all too easy to leave things until the last minute, a situation which must be avoided at all costs.

Timing is particularly important to the DIY shoot, as the periods available to do such work obviously have to be fitted in around career and family commitments, and is dependent upon organising a working party of sufficient shoot members. The time factor is just one reason why things should not be delayed – it goes without saying that once any rearing is begun and those other countless summer jobs around the shoot become a matter of priority, there may not be the time to make the best of your release pens.

Mending broken fences

If there has been serious winter or spring damage to the perimeter fencing, it is never an easy thing to cut the tree branches clear and re-attach the wire netting. A straining wire placed at the top of the fence is exactly that – there for straining – and, once broken, will never tighten again in the same way as it did when the pen was first constructed. It might, therefore pay to replace the damaged portion of the pen completely. If you have built it well, the undamaged sides should remain taut whilst repairs are being effected.

You will never, ever, succeed in pulling up wire-netting which has been stretched out of shape under the trunk or branch of a tree and so, despite the extra cost involved, replacing it with a roll of new netting, clipped tightly to a strand or two of replacement straining wire, is the sensible alternative. Instead of the tree damage being looked upon as a disadvantage, why not use it as a reason to extend the pen?

Re-pegging the base

Even if the pen itself requires no actual repairs, if the perimeter wire has been lifted during the season to allow access for beaters to blank it through into another drive, the base will benefit from being re-pegged in the spring rather than at the last minute, as this will allow new grass shoots to grow through the wire mesh and make the fence more secure by doing so.

If rabbits are plentiful, a few are probably living inside the pens where the wire has been lifted for access. It's not surprising really, as they will love the cover provided by the undergrowth and the easy feeding on the rides. Running a dog through the pen will help in pushing them back out before re-pegging the wire – there is nothing more frustrating than pegging down the wire only to find that, in doing so, you have effectively created a rabbit pen, the occupants of which continually try to burrow out.

Keeping the fence clear of growth

Even if you have been lucky enough not to have suffered any damage, some general

As well as the perimeter fence, overgrown anti-fox grids will need clearing of vegetation prior to the first batch of poults being released – and electric fences will probably require mending and tightening.

work in and around the pens should take place, preferably in the spring.

Branches and bushes both inside and outside the pen have a habit of growing! What was a good bit of low roosting last year may now be overhanging the fence line, making it an easy matter for newly-released birds to scramble out and predators to scramble in. These offending branches can be seen more easily at this time of year and will also be less likely to prove difficult to pull away once cut than they will in the early summer months when the leaves and new shoots are all intermingled.

Making improvements for the future

Inside the pen a little bit of coppicing or sky-lighting might allow the poults more sunning areas in which to bathe, scratch and dust. By waiting for a sunny day it can be seen over what parts of the pen the sun shines strongest and the canopy from these parts removed. In a couple of seasons, the coppiced pieces will have grown to provide intermediate roosting and replace existing easily-accessible branches which may have died off by then.

Try and remember any problem points you had last summer with birds which had flown out of the pen being unable to find an anti-fox funnel through which to return. It is easy when building a new pen, to place these funnels and grilles in what you think are strategic places at the base of the perimeter fencing, only to find that, as you attempt to walk them back in during the morning and evening feeds, poults refuse to run along the wire and veer off into a particularly thick patch of cover on the outside of the pen. An extra funnel may prevent this happening and also you from pulling out your hair in frustration.

The Day Before Release

If birds are released fully-winged (see 'To Clip or Not to Clip' later in this chapter), the anti-fox funnels will need to be open from the start, but otherwise, it may pay you to close the funnels of pens containing clipped birds for the first couple of days as, stupid though pheasants may appear to be, they are quite good at finding their way out through the wire mesh funnels.

On a similar matter: check all around the perimeter fence immediately before releasing any birds. Even though you may have checked a short time before, there is still the possibility that even where the bottom of a fence has been turned out and securely pegged, a rabbit may have opened up a fresh hole under the wire or a branch has fallen over the wire.

Releasing Time

If the weather is wet on the day you choose to take your birds to wood, it is certainly a good idea to hold off until it improves. If you are experiencing a spell of hot weather in July (which is, arguably, when the majority of the season's poults will be released) then you might need to think matters differently. Birds can soon overheat in hot weather and it is a sensible precaution to cut down on the numbers being carried in each crate.

The benefits of making an early start

Irrespective of weather conditions, it is always best if the poults are in the pens just as soon as is practicable, as this will give them the whole day to explore their new surroundings as well as find the food and water sources (of which there should be plenty). It will also give them chance to settle down quietly on their first night rather than just 'jug' on the ground wherever they find themselves as dusk draws in – as is quite likely to be the case if they were taken to wood in the late afternoon or early evening.

Crating birds up the night before and leaving them on a concrete floor in an airy out-building will help towards an early start the next morning, but for those whose birds are being brought in from game farms, the time of day the pheasants reach the pens is dictated by the travelling distance from game supplier to woodland release pen.

Obviously techniques differ depending on whether you are releasing pheasants or partridge but, no matter what, the same amount of care is needed when taking them to release pens: aim to have them there as early in the morning as possible in order to give them the whole day to settle in. In this particular situation, take note of the hopper to the left of the photo – and of the scrubby cover that will give extra security once the partridges are released (photo courtesy of Mike Swan).

Take time and care

Poults will adapt best to the pen if they are allowed to walk out from the carrying crates in their own time and this should be no problem when releasing birds you've reared yourself. Releasing birds supplied and brought in by a third party may not be as easy, as, understandably, the driver may wish to deliver and get away as quickly as possible. To do so, he or she needs the crates back on the trailer or van and may encourage you to rush and physically lift or push the pheasants out.

Place the crates with their side openings close to cover rather than down the centre of an open ride on which poults will feel vulnerable as they walk out from the crates. With several crates to unload, it should be possible to start near the gate and place them in a long line – by the time you have reached the spot for the last crate, the early ones will be empty and can be carried back to the trailer whilst the birds from the others are still finding their way into the cover.

Always make sure that food and water have been put in situ before the poults are released as it is important that they find the designated eating and drinking stations immediately upon beginning to explore their new surroundings. Also, you do not want to be disturbing them any more than is necessary by subsequently wandering about filling up hoppers.

To Clip or Not to Clip

The general view regarding wing clipping has changed: whereas, in the past, most, if not all keepers would wing clip their birds on transference to the release pens, the thinking nowadays is that clipping adds to the stress of release and can increase disease risk during release. Now that we have fewer drugs available, there can be very real problems in treating post-release disease. Also, huddles of wing-clipped poults roosting on the ground are highly vulnerable to anything that gets into the pen.

Not wing clipping has the advantage of ensuring that young pheasants are able to fly out of danger from the very first day, but much depends on the area and topography. There would, for instance, be little hope of keeping birds from flying straight out of a release pen built on the side of a steep hill, or in which there is little ground cover. In the first instance, a good majority would be straight over the wire at the first sign of any predator disturbance and in the second, they may even fly out on being released from the crates if it is not possible for them to quietly walk into the seclusion of low cover such as brambles or nettles.

Assuming that, for one reason or another, wing clipping is considered necessary, the following method applies.

Just clip one wing

Only one wing is clipped – the idea being to throw the bird off-balance if it attempts to fly. Clipping the wing is not difficult on a six-week-old bird: most if not all of the ten primary feathers will be juvenile and will be replaced by strong, mature ones in the next week or two. If birds cannot be released until later, perhaps because of bad weather, for instance, cutting the full amount will mean clipping some adult feathers which may not be replaced until the following season's moult. This will make the poults more vulnerable and could affect their flying capabilities.

It is easy enough to cut around the newly formed adult feathers – obvious by their blood quills and formation – but if it then only becomes possible to cut four or five of the ten, is there much point?

Even if you decide not to wing-clip, you might still like to consider wing-tagging birds with different coloured tags. This will enable you to record many factors: for example, whether poults from one particular pen do better than others – and how far they wander, if a new strain introduced to the shoot does better than the old one and, provided that the tags are printed with a year date, how old birds are when you catch them up (or shoot them) in subsequent seasons (photo courtesy of Mike Swan).

CHAPTER 8

Feeding Matters

The regular fluctuation in cereal prices will undoubtedly affect the cost of game rearing and any increase in wholesale costs to the feed manufacturer will, of course, be passed on to you! The costs of crumbs, pellets and other compounds are generally one of the greatest, if not *the* greatest, additions to the annual budget and so every effort must be made to use food sparingly and efficiently without, at the same time, causing your birds to suffer. Basically, it all comes down to whether one hopper feeds or hand feeds once the birds have been released, but long before then there is the feeding of laying birds and chicks on the rearing field to consider.

In the Laying Pen

Ad-lib feed hoppers containing breeder pellets are far less wasteful and more hygienic than if you were to choose to feed pheasants or partridges twice daily as a scatter feed directly on the floor. All gamebirds, no matter what their age, must have access to adequate supplies of clean, fresh drinking water at all times and the

---

What's the difference between hand and hopper feeding?

Hand feeding is simply the practice of scattering feed along rides at regular intervals – usually once, but sometimes twice, a day. Hoppers, depending on their size and the amount of birds being fed, only need checking and topping up on a regular rather than daily basis and can be invaluable on part-time keepered or DIY shoots. They can be commercially manufactured specifically for the purpose of feeding game, but more often are home constructed from cleaned-out drums or containers found around the farmyard. If hopper feeding, set out plenty of hoppers to begin with so that your game won't have to look for them – you can always reduce the numbers later on. In the opinion of most, hand feeding at regular times is much better than hopper feeding when it's important to hold birds exactly where you want them.

---

provision of drinkers should be sufficient to allow the birds adequate space to obtain water with minimum disturbance and competition. Automatic drinkers will also go a long way towards preventing the spread of disease among birds, not least because they are far less likely to become contaminated by their faeces.

On the Rearing Field

Key factors in the feeding of very young birds include the protein content and medicinal components in their ration which help combat coccidiosis and other disease challenges that may well pose a threat in the early weeks.

It is best to start with a crumb specifically designed for game bird rearing as they generally have a very high protein content before gradually moving birds onto a mini-pellet some time around two to three weeks of age. The size of the pellet is very important if wastage is to be avoided and, depending from whom you buy your feedstuffs, there are various options that will take the birds up to, and beyond, release stage. By this time, the protein content will obviously be lowered

An ad-lib feeder is useful in the laying pen, release pen and at feeding points around the shoot. Although it is possible to purchase several designs of attachments through which game birds can have access to the food, this particular one is fitted with a 'spiral': the birds very quickly learn that all they have to do is to reach up and peck at the coil which will scatter feed everytime it is touched (photo courtesy of Patrick Pinker game farms and equipment suppliers).

but pellets are, in my opinion, still very necessary and you should not be tempted into putting release-aged birds onto wheat at this stage in an effort to cut down on costs.

Water on the rearing field
Very young chicks are notorious for managing to drown themselves in the smallest amount of water. There are many chick drinkers on the market, most of them of the plastic twist-lock type, but personally I don't think you can beat the tried and trusted old-fashioned inverted jam-jar drinker.

Pellets are the mainstay of a game bird's early diet and are formulated in various sizes and with varying amounts of proteins and essential nutrients depending on the age of the birds to which they are being fed.

Drinkers for very young chicks
They must obviously be shallow enough that young chicks cannot fall in and the jam-jar drinker as manufactured by Eltex is a very safe drinker. All such drinkers work on the vacuum principle but simple is most definitely best in this instance: do not be tempted into purchasing the large type with integral handles as the 'trough' part is still too deep for very young chicks. Choose instead the ones where a standard jam jar fits into the galvanised base – even so, they are not foolproof and it will pay to cut a small piece of very thin hose that fits into the base of the trough and makes the available water level even shallower. Experienced keepers suggest using small clean pebbles to achieve the same purpose, but doing so is more time-consuming when it comes to cleaning out and replenishing the drinker.

Automatic drinkers
The Broiler Equipment Company (BEC) was founded in the UK over 50 years ago and is credited with developing the first round plastic automatic drinker for both poultry and game bird rearing. Since then, many other automatic drinkers suitable for both the rearing field and release pen have come on the market. Drinkers for very young poults are usually placed on the ground, but other types are designed to

be suspended, and, to prevent them swinging around, often have the option of being fitted with a sand or water ballast weight. A variation of the type can also be used in the release pens – provided, that is, there is a source of water available, usually from a header tank.

Some of the drinkers intended for use on the floor can be supplied with a 'chick-saver' ring which helps prevent chicks from drowning in their first few days of life. Nipple drinkers are another option – although they are mainly used in the poultry industry.

A feed consumption guide for the first six weeks	
0–7 days	1 bag per 1,000 birds per week
7–21 days	6 bags per 1,000 birds per week
21–31 days	10 bags per 1,000 birds per week
31 to release pen stage	15 bags per 1,000 birds per week

In the Release Pen

Release is a very stressful time for both pheasants and partridge, so it is a mistake to reduce the quality of feed at this stage. The birds may well be growing feathers as well as increasing bodyweight so to cut the protein down by changing from pellets to wheat or a cereal combination would be counter-productive. It is also important to maintain the protection from disease and ensure that vitamins and

Although old-fashioned jam-jar drinkers are perfect for young chicks, their use might not be practical when dealing with large numbers of birds – in which case, a series of gravity-fed automatic drinkers are ideal (photo courtesy of Alan Waugh/Stuart Fairhead/Heath Hatcheries).

trace elements are still available – which can only be done by the inclusion of pellets in their diet.

Make it an easy transition

If you have been using outdoor feeders and hoppers on the rearing field, try and use something similar in the release pens – there are many models on the market, most of which have a rain-cover that protects the feed in the tray from getting spoilt by rain. Using the same or similar designs makes it easier for young poults to identify the location of readily available food.

Even when you're intending to progress to hand feeding, a few feeders will help birds settle in over the first few days – you can then begin scattering food down the rides and gradually do away with the feeders. (If they are not needed elsewhere, remember to take them back to the yard, clean them and store them safely away just as soon as is practical; leaving them out in the wood is not good practice and they are liable to damage.)

Poults in the release pen being fed by a combination of hoppers and hand feeding. Note the water header tank to the left of the photo: it has been positioned on a stack of pallets due to the fact that the system is gravity-fed.

Introducing cereal feeds

Some grain feeding can begin not long after birds have been taken to the release pens but it's perhaps best to wait until they are around 10–12 weeks of age before including too much along with the pellets. The introduction of wheat should be brought about slowly. Maize, either whole or split (the latter is sometimes known as 'kibbled' in some parts of the country), can be used shortly afterwards, but always use it sparingly as it encourages birds to put on fat and may, in extreme cases, even prevent them from flying well.

Some feed manufacturers produce a treated cereal mix which looks a little like wild bird seed and is intended to be mixed with straight cereals in an effort to prevent your carefully reared stocks from straying too far.

Water in the release pen

Obviously the easiest way of ensuring a ready source of water is to include a running stream within the release pen, but this may create problems if, or more probably, when, any form of medication needs to be added in liquid form. Far better, then, to use the type of suspended drinkers which are gravity fed from header tanks than from, as is often seen, five-gallon drums split in half or, indeed, any other form of open vessel. Poults will adapt readily to such watering systems, as they will almost certainly have become used to them on the rearing field – especially if they have come from a commercial game farm.

The shoot budget may, nevertheless, leave many with no alternative but to make do with homemade open drinkers. In an ideal world, however, 'closed' drinkers keep cleaner, are less wasteful and certainly less susceptible to visitations from birds such as rooks, crows, pigeons or, in fact, small songbirds – any of which might spread unwanted disease.

Wheat and other cereals can be gradually introduced either as part of hand feeding...

...or via covered, weatherproof hoppers.

Suspended drinkers topped up from a header tank are probably the most convenient and hygienic automatic watering system for use both on the rearing field and, as is the case here, in the release pens.

On the Shoot

Personally, I've always preferred hand feeding, but I appreciate that time factors may leave many with no alternative other than to use hoppers in order to ensure that their partridges and pheasants get their daily ration.

Hoppers

The advocates of hopper feeding claim that some of the advantages can be seen in wilder birds and the fact that there's always food for the birds to find. The former I agree with; the latter I don't – and for a variety of reasons, not least of which is that, unless the hoppers are carefully maintained and watched, they can very quickly run empty or, whilst looking and feeling full, may be blocked at the distribution end, causing birds to go hungry and possibly wander off.

Disadvantages to hopper feeding

One of the great disadvantages to hopper feeding is the waste of food. Small hoppers can be knocked over on a regular basis by deer and the contents eaten. Any homemade equipment will, unless carefully constructed with galvanised metal, soon be chewed through by squirrels. Rats love an easy meal and, as can often be seen, soon take up residence on any feed ride, especially in close proximity to hoppers.

When wheat and other cereals were cheap to purchase, perhaps this type of wastage could be tolerated, but now, what with today's prices and the promise of them escalating even further, any amount of waste and spoilt food will add dramatically to the shoot budget. Of course, it may be possible to keep such wastage to a minimum by instigating a springtime offensive against rats, squirrels and birds such as rooks and crows and continuing with a judicious programme throughout the rearing season and into the autumn.

Making your own hoppers

Homemade hoppers have, though, stood the test of time and it is possible to purchase several designs of attachments through which gamebirds can have access to the food. Possibly the most common one to be seen is the 'spiral': the birds very quickly learn that all they have to do is to reach up and peck at the coil which will scatter feed every time it is touched. It sometimes happens that badgers and deer learn to steal from spiral feeders and cause damage to the spiral or coil whilst doing so. To avoid this, it is possible to buy SBD Guards and T Bars.

Wright feeder nozzles are another alternative, but the way the feed is held beneath the hoppers means that compound pellets can quite easily become damp and so it is best only to use these types of hopper when feeding cereals such as wheat or kibbled maize. Mac Feeder nozzles have four slots running vertically down the outside of the feeding nozzle and a further two around its base – not only is the feed protected from the weather to such an extent that pellets do not become damp, but the layout of the slots means that birds certainly do have to work for their food, making them less inclined to wander.

Regular hopper maintenance

If through choice or circumstances, you have decided to favour hopper feeding in its various forms and, assuming that you have managed to dissuade vermin of whatever kind from destroying them, they require a little maintenance. You should, however, do more than give them a cursory glance, or, as I have seen so often, a sideways kick when checking them.

Taking the lid off to see how much grain the hopper contains is elementary but, depending on the system used to allow game to feed, you also need to check that the spiral, pendulum or whatever distribution mechanism is fitted, has not become blocked by damp food.

Move them a few yards every so often in order that the ground beneath does not become a muddy mess caused by the birds' feet and constant pecking, and, in areas where deer are plentiful, it may pay to tie them to a tree or fence post so that they are not forever being knocked over.

Paint your hoppers!

If you have the time, paint your hoppers so that they are more in keeping with the countryside and are less visible. If they are too obvious, they might attract the unwanted attentions of people walking along a nearby footpath and may be knocked over out of devilment. Also, the fact that the hoppers are noticed could cause people to explore the surrounding area and discover pheasant release pens or partridge sections which would otherwise have gone undetected. A coat of animal-friendly paint every season helps in protecting hoppers from the elements and even galvanised ones will benefit from such treatment.

Many keepers nowadays use a type of trailer fitted with a spinner attachment pulled by an ATV as a means of feeding their birds out in the game crops and woodland.

Water on the shoot

The provision of clean water across the shoot is as important as the provision of feed and yet water supplies outside the release area often receive little attention or investment. The importance of water is perhaps better emphasised when you consider that 100, 14-week-old pheasant poults will drink around 10 litres of water a day, with 100 red-leg partridges consuming approximately half that amount.

During a dry summer and autumn, taking the trouble to keep drinkers topped up will help in ensuring that last year's birds remain in the vicinity even though they may, by now, be finding their own source of naturally occurring food. Once the season's poults are released, a good clean water supply is absolutely vital, not just in the release pen areas, but also along any hedgerows down which birds need to be encouraged towards shooting woodland or cover crops. To help pheasants and partridges become established in the cover crops, where possible, one should include some drinkers.

Grit

Whilst on the subjects of basics such as food and water, it is well worth also mentioning the provision of grit. Having no teeth, all birds need grit. Without the aid of insoluble grit, they would find it nearly impossible to make much use of their food, especially whole-grains. Flint grit is essential in allowing birds to digest food once it has entered the gizzard. Because stones on the ground are usually rounded, any that are found naturally have little effect on grinding food into the necessary consistency, so it is not a bad idea to include a little extra at most feeding stations as well as in the breeding, rearing and release pens.

Grit is also a means of supplying calcium and although this is often included in manufactured feedstuffs, it can be given separately as oyster shell or ground limestone. There are some who say that, when fed on a balanced pelleted food, the extra addition is unnecessary and could, in fact, be harmful. Having reared game for over 30 years and all manner of poultry for even longer, I must say that I would rather risk including extra grit than the possibility of not providing enough.

Straw Bales on the Feed Ride

If you can still get them, a line of small bales along a hedge, perhaps interspersed with feed hoppers, will help in attracting pheasant poults towards game crops and woodland cover. From personal experience, I found that a line of such bales placed two high are much favoured by both pheasants and French partridge, which will use them as 'look-out' points.

If you are using small bales along a feed ride, line them out at strategic distances apart, but do not spread them out. By leaving them for a while so that the birds can jump up on them and peck and scratch around their base, they will last much longer. After a time, and before the bales become too soggy, remove the strings and let the pheasants scratch them out themselves: it saves you a job and keeps them entertained for longer, especially if a daily ration of corn is scattered around the bales.

Spring feeding

In the spring, once there is some natural feed appearing for the birds, you could store the hoppers until they are needed again for the coming season's birds, but in many cases, they would be better being moved to the woodland edge or positioned along a nearby hedge to help in encouraging birds to breed and contribute to any wild stock. Pheasants and partridges in good condition will obviously be more successful than those whose feed source has been taken away just as soon as shooting has finished. Locate them in such a way that as much of the shoot as possible is covered and certainly where cocks begin to collect a harem of hens.

CHAPTER 9

Disease and Medication

Some medications such as Emtryl (dimetridazole), for instance, are, under EU legislation implemented during the first decade of this century, no longer legal to use. Therefore, should you have any shooting and gamekeeping books published before, let's say, 2005, their recommendations as to what medicines to use might well prove erroneous.

Another point worth mentioning is that while some medications are legally available, they may not be authorised for use in certain situations (see '"Cascade" Regulations' later in this chapter). It is best if you take advice from your vet, or from the up-to-date information to be found on websites of the BASC, NGO and the Game Farmers' Association. The information contained within this chapter is legal and applicable at the time of writing but is as well to remember just how quickly things can change; for instance, it seems that the EU is currently attempting to ban any drugs that are designed to be included in food ... should you be reading this book some years after publication, it might, therefore, be advisable to check with your food producer or veterinary surgeon as regards the current situation (see also 'Veterinary Medicines Regulations' later in this chapter).

What to Do to Avoid Transmission of Disease

It's all a matter of commonsense. You should be constantly aware of the fact that the more birds there are reared in close proximity to one another, the more potential disease problems you are likely to encounter ... remember, the mark of a good keeper is, in the opinion of most vets, diligence.

Buy local

It's always prudent to buy your stock from a local supplier rather than from an unknown game farm miles away; it is vitally important that you know your source – and that they have a reputation for providing birds with a natural immunity built up over generations of careful disease-free breeding.

Feed the youngest first

If you keep stock of different ages (birds in a laying pen, poults on the rearing field), remember that most diseases are transmitted from the oldest to the youngest: therefore see to your youngest birds first.

Dip your boots

It is worth considering a foot dip at strategic points (at the entrance to the laying pen, the incubator shed, etc.). BioVX or similar will help, but always ensure you remove the worst of the dirt from your boots with a stiff brush prior to dipping. You should also change the dipping solution according to the manufacturer's instructions and not on an ad-hoc basis.

Keep equipment clean

You must clean the incubators and hatchers after every hatch and the rearing sheds after use (another clean prior to the first time they are used the following season won't come amiss either). Use an approved disinfectant such as Rhodasept to help eliminate bacteria, viruses and fungal spores (pathogens). Don't forget that feeders and drinkers are one of the worst disease transmitters so keep them clean at all times.

In an effort to keep disease at bay, every effort should be made to keep drinkers and feeders as scrupulously clean as possible – easier said than done when young game birds seem to like nothing more than perching on such things and defecating into feed and water! (photo courtesy of Alan Waugh/Stuart Fairhead/Heath Hatcheries).

Wage war on vermin

Rats and mice are big carriers of diseases such as salmonella. Keeping grass short in and around runs and sheds will not only lessen the chance of fungal disease such as aspergillosis, but also deprive rats and mice of cover. Keep feed in sealed containers and place poison-baiting stations in appropriate places (see also Chapter 4).

Diseases and Prevention

Any game bird can be continually challenged by different diseases but with good biosecurity and a watchful eye, the potential for disease problems is lessened. However, it is extremely unlikely that you will get through your gamekeeping career without encountering some pathogens so it is as well to know what to look for.

Keep stressors (e.g. lack of shelter in wet weather, bullying, not enough feeders or drinkers, predator or vermin presence) as low as possible. Provide preventative treatment with Detoxerol (electrolytes and vitamins), Herban (oregano-based pathogen inhibitor) or cider vinegar (acidifies water controlling pathogens) at release or at stressful times. When considering cider vinegar it is important to only use plastic or stainless steel drinkers since the acid will leach toxic zinc from galvanised drinkers (the cider vinegar dose rate is 10ml per 500ml of water).

Worms and worming

All game birds are at risk from parasitic worms and, according to some vets, gamekeepers need to take their worming programmes far more seriously than they do. The risk of infection builds up year on year if birds are left untreated and a significant worm burden can result in all sorts of problems. Worm eggs and larvae occur naturally in the environment, inside earthworms, insects and wild birds (which are intermediate hosts or carriers).

Worm eggs are liable to live in the soil for years and are resistant to disinfectants. Contaminated soil and dirty rearing field litter can harbour both eggs and larvae.

Syngamus trachea

Better known amongst gamekeepers and the shooting world as 'gapeworm', this particular worm lives in the bird's windpipe and can so badly affect this part of the anatomy that the bird chokes – hence the gaping for breath and the name. Clinical signs may, however, vary in birds, from the typical outstretched neck and open beak as a bird attempts to breathe, to a cough, shaking of the head and a 'snicking' sound as the bird attempts to remove the windpipe obstruction. In a few cases these typical signs are not present and affected birds simply lose condition and may die with few respiratory signs being seen.

Infection is via the oral route, with earthworms and other soil-living creatures being the worm hosts. The periodic moving of rearing fields and release pens will help in preventing too great a build-up, but this isn't always practical or possible.

Treating parasitic worms

If you are a professional or large-scale producer of game birds, it makes sense to have Flubenvet or similar added to your compound foods by the manufacturer. Smaller flocks can, since October 2011, be protected against parasitic worm infections by use of the 240g Keeper Pack of Flubenvet which can be dispensed by a vet without a Category 8 mixing licence – as long as the recipient is using it for domestic use. It can be useful to have in case of an outbreak, but in-feed by the compounder is by far the easier route, especially at release due to the stress of travelling suppressing the immune system.

Animal wormers intended for use on farmyard livestock are sometimes suggested as being suitable for worming game birds – many of which are. However, under the Veterinary Medicines Regulations, using such products not specifically licensed for a condition in a particular species might well be illegal without a prescription from your veterinary surgeon so it is best to take professional advice on this.

It is also important to mention the need to use the correct dosage: resistance to wormers is a huge issue and one of the worst things you can do is under-dose. By giving a low dose the parasites that have a degree of resistance are able to survive (they would be killed with a suitable dose) and they then breed. Resistance to anthelmintics (wormers) is just as serious as antibiotic resistance (see 'Resistance to Antibiotics' below).

Gapeworms in the trachea (windpipe) of a pheasant (photo courtesy of Victoria Roberts, BVSc MRCVS).

An example of intestines that have become impacted with roundworms (photo courtesy of Victoria Roberts, BVSc MRCVS).

Coccidiosis

Even though most manufactured crumbs have an anti-coccidiostat included, it is important to realise that coccidiostats are inhibitors, rather than eradicators, allowing the young birds a trickle infection to stimulate immunity. But you always need to be on the look-out for signs of coccidiosis in young game bird chicks. The first obvious signs may well be watery yellow droppings, weight loss, ruffled feathers and a hunched appearance, usually with the wings drooping. Birds can die very rapidly if the disease is not checked so it's important to make the correct diagnosis as quickly as possible (a post-mortem of affected live birds is far better than taking already dead ones to the vet). Internal examination will most likely show that the caeca contains evidence of watery yellow fluid, milky white fluid or hard caecal cores.

There are three species of coccidia that can affect pheasants: *Eimeria colchici, Eimeria phasiani* and *Eimeria duodenalis*. Partridges are also susceptible to a fourth species, *Eimeria legionensis* which, if contracted, can result in very high mortality. Drugs containing toltrazuril or amprolium are likely to be recommended in the face of an outbreak, but again, prevention by acidifying the water is useful.

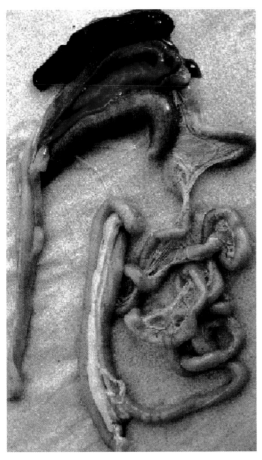

Birds can die very rapidly if coccidiosis is not quickly identified – a post-mortem of affected live birds is far better than taking already dead ones to the vet. Here the caeca can be seen to be severely affected (photo courtesy of Victoria Roberts, BVSc MRCVS).

Mycoplasmosis

Often referred to as 'Swelly Eye' or 'Bulgy Eye' by gamekeepers, the scientifically correct name is *Mycoplasma gallisepticum* which is a respiratory pathogen affecting both poultry and game birds. The disease is most often seen in adult birds, though all ages may be affected; in fact, research on pheasants has shown that it can infect young pheasants at one day old or adults at 20 weeks. Typically, mycoplasma bacterial infections are associated with respiratory problems which include severe sinusitis, sneezing/coughing, conjunctivitis, watery eye, nasal discharge, slow growth, leg problems and a marked reluctance to move and, when affecting adult birds, reduced hatchability and chick viability. It is highly contagious and can be carried in the air and/or on clothing but, crucially, it is transmitted through the egg from the parent stock, so this is another reason to know and trust your supplier's hygiene systems.

Various antibiotics have been used to treat mycoplasma infections including Tylan, tiamulin, tetracyclines and Linco-Spectin, but none was licensed specifically for use in pheasants or game birds. Recently though, a new

Mycoplasma is often referred to as 'swelly eye' or 'bulgy eye' by gamekeepers; you can see why in this example of a badly affected partridge (photo courtesy of Victoria Roberts, BVSc MRCVS).

oral antibiotic tylvalosin (Aivlosin) has received a full marketing authorisation through the European Regulatory Authorities and, according to practising vets, is 'presently working really well.' Keeping ammonia levels low in rearing sheds and using preventative treatment with Detoxerol, Herban or cider vinegar in the water is also beneficial.

Purely out of interest, but a matter for concern nevertheless, is the fact that it appears grouse are now contracting this disease in certain moorland areas – the reason given being that they are picking it up from red-legged partridges released on the lower moor edges.

Rotavirus

Rotavirus infection most often affects young poults between the age of three days and two weeks – although it has been seen in birds of all ages. At chick stage, it results in wet droppings and may cause vent pecking. Birds will also huddle together and, in a worse case scenario, some may well die within a few hours of the first clinical signs being noticed.

Whilst there is no specific treatment for rotavirus, affected birds should be given re-hydration salts via the water to prevent dehydration – using a water disinfectant that is effective against viruses, such as Virkon S, will prevent birds being infected from a contaminated water supply. In some cases, antibiotics may be effective against any secondary bacterial infections but will have no direct impact on the viral infection itself.

Hexamatosis

Hexamita is an intestinal parasite and can affect poults from the age of three weeks upwards – although experience tells me that it is most likely to be seen after the birds have been taken to the woodland release pens. As with coccidiosis, often the first signs are yellow diarrhoea and a lethargic nature; in fact, during the latter stages, it is possible to walk up to a bird and pick it up without it making any attempt to run away. If you do find a bird in this condition, its most obvious feature is a rapid and quite alarming weight loss – especially around the keel (breast) bone. Sometimes it is noticed that the bird's intake of food is increased, but before long they will go the other way and show no interest at all in feeding. Post-mortem examination, either by a vet or an experienced keeper, is essential in order to ensure that birds can be correctly diagnosed and treated straight away – again, live birds are better than dead ones as the parasite is not so easily seen after birds have been dead for a while.

Treatment is limited since the use of Emtryl was banned by the EU in the early part of the last decade; tetracyclines and tiamulin have, though, proved to be of use. Veterinary surgeons experienced in poultry and game bird disease tell me that electroytes and glucose can also be beneficial – especially when feed intake is low. Preventative treatment with Detoxerol, Herban or cider vinegar is also useful at release.

Coronavirus

Game birds are occasionally diagnosed as having coronavirus infections – of which there are many different strains. In adult breeding birds, the virus can often remain in the bird without causing any real harm until stress brought on by the onset of

Trichomonosis

Displaying similar symptoms to *hexamita*, *trichomonas* is in fact, a protozoa and also causes painful plaques in the mouth and throat. Ronidazole is the prefered treatment, but using cider vinegar will help in its prevention.

In October 2011, much was made in the media regarding some songbirds (notably greenfinches and chaffinches) succumbing to the 'new' disease of trichomonosis. Experts from various bird welfare organisations, who were interviewed on the subject, were of the opinion that the disease had only been known since about 2006. As far as keepers and game farmers are concerned, they have known of trichomonosis for a great deal longer than that. Wood pigeons are also known to carry trichomonosis – and it's possible that they will transmit the disease to game bird stocks. Raptor keepers call it 'frounce', mentioned in early falconry texts of hundreds of years ago.

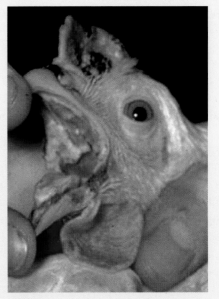

Seen here affecting the throat and mouth of a chicken, trichomonosis can be contracted by game birds – as well as songbirds and other wild species (photo courtesy of Victoria Roberts, BVSc MRCVS).

laying causes the virus to become virulent. Game farmers or keepers who use pheasants caught in the woods at the end of the shooting season should be particularly vigilant as these birds are more likely to suffer from or to be carrying the problem.

In an attempt to induce immunity in the birds, poultry vaccines have been used in the past but, as there are many distinct strains of coronavirus, it is not possible to ensure control with the limited number of suitable vaccines available. Pheasants may be vaccinated by eye-drop as they enter the laying pens.

In the opinion of most vets, and, according to website research, there is no medication available to control outbreaks of this disease and so good biosecurity is exceptionally important in order to prevent it spreading. Known infected birds – and all the birds in an affected breeding flock should be assumed to be infected – should not be released back into the wild as this will form a large reservoir of infection available to the next generation of breeding birds.

Brachyspira

Spirochaetes have long been known to colonise the intestines of some birds. Reports on potentially pathogenic brachyspira species have led to increased knowledge of the complexity of intestinal *spirochaetes* in avian species, especially poultry and game birds – a fortunate finding as brachyspira is currently being reported as an increasing problem in the game keeping and shooting world. Symptoms can include a failure to gain body weight, decreased body weight and mild to moderate diarrhoea (sometimes yellow and frothy). In poultry, it seems to be more common on multi-age sites so it makes sense to be extra vigilant in circumstances where breeding game birds are kept close to rearing units.

Treatments are limited to drinking water medications: notably tiamulin, valnemulin and chlortetracycline.

Aspergillosis

A fungus which can grow in long, moist grass in warm conditions, soiled damp floor litter and badly-kept food, aspergillosis is sometimes known as 'brooder pneumonia' and, as that particular name suggests, young chicks on the rearing field are particularly susceptible.

Contracted when the environment such as a lovely warm brooder shed becomes home to high levels of the fungal spores floating in the atmosphere, once infected, chicks will rarely recover as there is no reliable treatment (antibiotics will not help). Some vets might, however, suggest an antifungal such as Itraconazole.

By far your best method of avoiding this particular problem is to prevent the possibilities of it occurring. Keep the environment free of possible

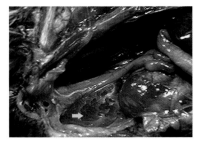

Air-sac affected by *aspergillus* plaques – which are indicated exactly in this photo by the yellow arrow (photo courtesy of Victoria Roberts, BVSc MRCVS).

spore-breeding places by cutting the long grass before you allow chicks out into the runs, remove daily any damp patches in the litter surrounding drinkers and feeders, make sure that chick crumbs are stored well and, most importantly, thoroughly clean and disinfect brooder sheds and incubators between each and every batch of birds.

Duck virus enteritis

Duck virus enteritis (DVE) is caused by a herpes virus and is most likely to be noticed during late spring or early summer. It can affect reared mallard of all ages, ranging from week-old ducklings right through to mature birds and, depending on the age, may show itself in many ways. The first signs are often a loss of appetite, ruffled feathers, soiled vents, watery diarrhoea and some nasal discharge.

Affected birds might struggle to keep their balance – often attempting to use their wings for support. In ducklings, symptoms can also include dehydration, loss of weight and bloodstained vents. In laying stock there is also likely to be a significant drop in egg production (but this is not always the case). DVE can be carried without symptoms by free-flying wild waterfowl, so preventing these from mixing with ducklings is sensible.

If you suspect birds of having succumbed to this disease in the past, contact your veterinary surgeon as they may be able to suggest the use of a live vaccine.

Avian influenza ('bird flu')

It is impossible to state with any degree of certainty as to what you should do about 'bird flu' as any such outbreak will be taken on its merits and instructions given to those concerned by the relevant DEFRA department. Typically, this could involve 'exclusion zones' around a place where an outbreak is suspected – or, in a worst case scenario, involve the total culling of affected birds. Look for the latest disease status on www.defra.gov.uk

A Word About Vaccines

Vaccines, many of which are not licensed for use in pheasants and so their use in such a situation might well be technically illegal, use live attenuated or naturally mild strains of virus and may sometimes be helpful in gradually eradicating some strains of disease. However, breeding and productivity might well be affected and, in the opinion of many, vaccinated birds are never as strong as those that have been kept under normal conditions and are naturally healthy. Veterinary surgeon and game bird disease expert Mark Elliot has this to say on the matter:

> We arguably do not have any good vaccines specifically for pheasants yet; the vaccines we use come from chicken and turkey industries and are given in hope that they produce the protection required. Vaccinating pheasants with live virus may risk introducing the problem rather than solving it.

So what should we do? ... We should lobby the pharmaceutical industry to produce more specific vaccines for game birds, based on researched need. In my view, we should not, unless absolutely necessary (and then only with more data on efficacy), be using live chicken and turkey vaccines for game birds. Vaccine use must be targeted correctly to the species, be safe and effective, and not add risk to the industry.

The good news is that some useful vaccines, already in development, should soon appear. One much needed is a specific coccidiosis vaccine and this is most likely to be the first specifically for game birds.

Examples of sick pheasant chicks: watery yellow droppings, weight loss, ruffled or wet-looking feathers, drooping wings and a hunched appearance might well indicate coccidiosis – but could equally be a symptom of something else. It is crucial that the correct diagnosis is made as quickly as possible (photo courtesy of Victoria Roberts, BVSc MRCVS).

Prescription-only Medications

Medications added to proprietary game feeds are almost always supplied as prescription-only medications – POM-V (veterinarian) – and as such, unless the feed manufacturers have their own 'in-house' vet, you may be required to visit your own as to procure the necessary paperwork before they can legally mix and supply a batch for your shoot.

Dosage and Administration

When medication is given via the water supply, there are many things to remember – just four of which are mentioned here:

1. Rates to administer vary depending on the size of the birds and so need to be adjusted according to age.

2. No other water should be available – a difficult task during spells of bad weather.

3. Depending on what is being administered, a fresh medicated solution should probably be provided once a day; others may require more. It is recommended that Baycox®, for instance, should be made up twice daily in hard water areas and in hot weather.

4. Some medications are not successful in hard water areas due to the pH levels affecting their efficiency.

A Rough Guide to Water Consumption

At day-old, 1,000 pheasants will drink 9 litres (2gal) of water daily and 1,000 red-legged partridges half that amount. This ratio remains pretty constant no matter what the age of pheasant/partridge so, for the remainder of this list, for partridges assume half the quantities given here for pheasants.

Pheasant age	Daily consumption (1,000 birds)
1 day	9 litres (2gal)
1 week	13 litres (3.5gal)
2 weeks	20 litres (5gal)
3 weeks	27 litres (7gal)
4 weeks	40 litres (10.5gal)
5 weeks	54 litres (14gal)
6 weeks	60 litres (16gal)
7 weeks	64 litres (17gal)
8 weeks	68 litres (18gal)
9 weeks	73 litres (19gal)
10 weeks	as above
11 weeks	78 litres (20.5gal)
12 weeks	as above
Adult	110 litres (29gal)

NB: These quantities are all approximate, and will fluctuate throughout the season, dependent mainly on the weather.

'Cascade' Regulations

A veterinary surgeon might well talk of prescribing drugs under 'cascade regulations'. DEFRA point out that the main aim is to 'provide a veterinary surgeon (and only a veterinary surgeon) with an important derogation from the general restrictions on the use of veterinary medicines'. They go on to say that, 'outside of a veterinary surgeon's prescription, the use of medicines must be strictly in accordance with the conditions of the marketing authorisation and the label directions should be closely followed' and explain:

> When the European legislation was drafted it was recognised that the veterinary market for medicines is small in comparison to that for human medicines and therefore it is likely that there would be many diseases where veterinary medicines would be unavailable. Thus, when there is no suitable medicine available, the cascade permits veterinary use of medicines intended for other clinical indications or species, specifically under the direction of a veterinary surgeon, thus recognising that the veterinarian is best placed to take the risk management decision associated with the use of an unauthorised medicine.

NB: A point well worth noting is that clients receiving medications via the cascade will need to sign a consent form for off-label use.

What are the Veterinary Medicines Regulations?

The Veterinary Medicinal Products Directive sets out the controls on the manufacture, authorisation, marketing, distribution and post-authorisation surveillance of veterinary medicines applicable in all European Member States. The Directive provides the basis for the UK controls on veterinary medicines, which are set out nationally in the Veterinary Medicines Regulations. The Regulations are revoked and replaced on an annual basis after consultation with interested groups to ensure that they are up-to-date and fit for purpose.

The latest Veterinary Medicines Regulations came into force on 1 October 2011 and, amongst other things, implement EU legislation relating to medicated feeds, and some specified feed additives used in feedstuffs.

Medication Reports

When a disease has been diagnosed and a course of action decided upon, your veterinary surgeon should provide you with a game bird medication report form – which is in your interest to complete. On it will be found places to record some or all of the following information:
• Date of administration
• Name and quantity of medication used
• Name/initials of person administering the medicine
• Estate name/flock identification
• Date treatment finished
• Date withdrawal period ended

- Name of prescribing veterinary surgeon
- Batch number
- Expiry date (of medication).

A veterinary post-mortem is the only way of correctly identifying many diseases. Histomonosis (sometimes known as 'Blackhead') will sometimes show as lesions on the liver of game birds (photo courtesy of Victoria Roberts, BVSc MRCVS).

Resistance to Antibiotics

According to a government report published in 2007, over 53 percent of antibiotics used in the UK are given to animals, mostly in food or water. About 90 percent of veterinary antibiotic use is in farm animals.

Excessive antibiotic use in farm animals (and this includes game birds) may lead to higher levels of antibiotic resistance, which can have consequences for animal health and welfare, as diseases become untreatable, and for human health, when resistant bacteria transfer from animals to humans.

Use antibiotics sparingly – and never without diagnosis

There is a tendency to use antibiotics far too regularly in the laying pen, on the rearing field and even at post-release. While such things are good, they can, when used indiscriminately, simply serve to mask the real problem. Antibiotics should always only ever be seen as a control measure and will not under normal circumstances eradicate a particular disease. Resistance to antibiotics is a real and serious problem.

In 2011, Joyce D'Silva, from Compassion in World Farming said: 'Unfortunately in the UK as in Europe and across the world, antibiotics are still being given to healthy stock as a cheap insurance policy against possible disease, often in the feed or drink of whole herds and flocks of livestock.'

Poisons and Accidental Poisoning

The unintentional poisoning of both birds and animals around the shoot is a constant worry and should be something of which all involved are aware.

• If crumbs contain lasalocid as a coccidiostat, ensure that these are kept away from dogs as lasalocid is extremely toxic to them and can, in fact, prove fatal. Additionally, some coccidiostats known as 'ionophores' are toxic to guinea fowl, so if you are using these birds as watch-dogs around the release pen (as many keepers do), it is important to check feed content.

• It is perhaps obvious to say that rat poison should not be placed close to anywhere dogs and game birds have access, but beware of the possibility of the rats themselves carrying poison into open places – remember too, to dispose of any rat bodies carefully (and legally).

• Also beware of agricultural chemicals, dressed seed and even spilt battery acid, which, like toxic anti-freeze, has a taste that animals and birds seem to like.

• Poisoning can also be produced by a toxin originating from a fungus found in foodstuffs such as nuts, sunflower seeds and grain that have been stored in warm, humid conditions. Known as 'aflatoxicosis', symptoms can include a lack of appetite, general lethargy, haemorrhage, and liver and kidney failure, so do not be tempted into dumping piles of spoilt and musty-smelling 'tailings' around the shoot in the fond hope that it will give the birds something in which to peck around and scratch. It will, but maybe at some cost.

• Pheasants and partridges are normally sensible about what they can and cannot eat and I have, in the past, watched with alarm whilst pheasants, in particular, have pecked away at fallen yew berries, which, as almost everyone knows, are deadly poisonous. In actual fact, the flesh of the berry is not, and it is only the seeds therein that are. Therefore, one can only assume that the reason pheasants and indeed all other wild birds remain unaffected after ingesting them is because the seeds pass through the body untouched.

Gizzard Impaction

When functioning normally, a bird's gizzard grinds down food materials in order to reduce their size and aid digestion. Gizzard activity also acts as a pacemaker of intestinal activity and controls the speed at which food is passed to the small intestine.

Gizzard impaction is generally caused by the gizzard and/or crop becoming bound with litter, grass, string or other foreign matter. This condition usually affects only a small number of birds; however, if young chicks do not begin to eat feed properly they often consume litter instead and may become impacted.

In situations where chicks are suspected of dying from this problem, you can do a post-mortem yourself: on opening, the gizzard will be found to contain a mass of fibrous material which may extend into the proventriculus (acid-producing stomach) and on into the duodeunum (small intestine). There is, sadly, no treatment and good brooding management, adequate feed and water is the best way of avoiding the problem.

CHAPTER 10

Game Crops and How to Use Them

In over thirty years of contributing to various sporting magazines, I have written much on the subject of game crops – so much so that you wouldn't think that there was anything new left to say. However, although a traditional and important mainstay of many shoots, game crops are, or at least should be, ever-changing and improving as farming research improves, government grants become available (or are withdrawn!) and new types of possible and potential varieties of seeds are tried, tested and found to be successful.

The Value of Game Crops

I would guess that the majority of shoots in the UK rely on game crops to provide at least half of their shooting, especially in the early part of the season when it is advantageous to keep the woodlands as a sanctuary. Partridge shoots would probably not be able to exist without the inclusion of some game cover situated in such a way that birds can be driven into the crop before being flushed out again in order to provide the waiting Guns with a fast-flying and exciting challenge.

Of particular value is the fact even the smallest strip can be of great use when planted along a hedge or even a barbed wire fence as it will undoubtedly help in drawing birds from one part of the shoot to another and also offer an ideal feeding and sunning place during the early autumn.

Holding birds in cold weather can be a major problem for many shoots – a problem which can often be addressed by good game crop planning. The right sort of game crops can also be used as a windbreak along the edge of an exposed shelter belt or even to prevent prying eyes from seeing the location of a release pen should a public right-of-way happen to run close by.

Making the Most of What the Farmer Plants

Depending on what has been sown, it does, of course, make sense to make the most of any conveniently placed crops grown by the farmer as winter sheep or cattle fodder.

Maize is useful, but will be harvested in October and so if you're going to make a drive of it, you need to do so on your first day's shooting. Including it then might mean that you can leave some of the woods and hedgerows until later.

Kale is robust enough to last all season and if it is a crop grown for cattle, it might work best if, with the farmer's permission, you can wait until he has either cut or strip-grazed the kale into a size more manageable to beaters and Guns.

Any large field of crops is difficult to drive even with beaters and dogs as game will run back between the beating line rather than flush forward towards the waiting Guns. Although you might manage to get a few of them to take off, such is the safety and security offered by a large field of cover that they will merely fly back over the heads of the walking line, or skim out to the sides.

Set-aside cover for partridge

- By establishing a seed-rich game crop in the spring and maintaining it for two years, you can provide natural food and cover throughout the winter at a low cost. Kale and quinoa are particularly useful components in the mix.
- You can also establish brood-rearing cover in the autumn. Use a mix of a cereal and a brassica such as mustard or linseed, and up to 5 percent red clover to attract insects. Establishing this adjacent to a tussocky grass margin creates an insect-rich chick feeding area. Maintain this for two years to provide seed in the second winter.
- The natural regeneration of rotational set-aside provides more seed food over winter than non-rotational set-aside.
- If possible, delay the use of a broad-spectrum herbicide until July. This will provide important feeding and nesting habitat in the spring. Alternatively, 20m strips of non-rotational set-aside can provide nesting habitat. Cut on or just before 15 August and make use of the option to leave 25 percent uncut for up to three years.

Kale is grown by many farmers as winter feed and can prove a useful asset on many shoots ... but it is not always appreciated by the beaters though as walking through it can be a miserable experience on a wet day! (photo courtesy of Richard Barnes/Kings Game Cover).

Stewardship schemes and grant aid

Always be on the look-out for the possibilities of grants when it comes to planting game crops. The various schemes are numerous – and often confusing: it is very easy to get your Environmental Stewardship Scheme, Countryside Stewardship Scheme and Environmentally Sensitive Areas mixed up with your Entry Level Scheme, Organic Entry Level Scheme, Higher Level Scheme and Single Payment Scheme, so it is perhaps best to consult with your local DEFRA offices, a knowledgeable agronomist or an advisor from the Game Conservation and Wildlife Trust!

The Positioning of Game Cover

Large shooting estates are obviously in a more fortunate position than the rented ones when it comes to the positioning of game cover.

It may be that, for one reason or another, certain parts of the estate are unsuitable to be utilised for anything much as far as farming is concerned and remain fallow for much of the year. If such a place exists on your shoot, you might like to consider planting it with game cover. While the unfavourable soil structure might not encourage a really good crop, there will certainly be enough cover and interesting feeding and dusting places created to encourage birds to stay in the area rather than wander off over the boundary. If it does grow well, and if it is topographically suitable, it should be an easy matter to either mow rides through it or cut away certain blocks to provide some manageable early season drives.

For the smaller shoot, there is probably very little choice as far as the actual siting of a game crop is concerned: it will be the type of seed to be planted that causes the biggest headache. What is eventually used obviously depends on the soil structure, topography, likelihood of disease, attacks by rabbits and insects such as flea-beetle and likely weather damage so, although it might seem an unnecessary expense, the best bet is to employ the services of a qualified agronomist.

How big should my game crop be?

Small areas can be used to boost existing cover and to act as linking corridors between woodland cover. The size of a game crop depends on many variables: density of game birds, costs and availability of land are just three. The shape is also important. The GWCT recommend that, generally speaking, the width of a game crop should be governed by two factors: shelter from the wind inside the crop and the width of the beating line, allowing for a 5m gap between beaters in most crops. In addition, remember that to be eligible for a grant, a 'Wild Bird Cover' crop on set-aside land must have a minimum width of 20m (unless part of a whole field of set-aside) and a minimum area of 0.3ha. Many keepers would suggest that their ideal size for a really useful cover crop is between 1 and 3ha.

The size and positioning of any cover planted specifically for game should take things like topography into account. Here a natural slope and attractive nearby woodland is a guarantee of success.

What Crop?

Some crops supply feed alone, others offer just cover, whilst some provide both. Any one of the well-known and nationally respected game cover and conservation crops advisors, or your local agricultural seed suppliers, will be able to offer detailed help pertaining to your particular ground and topography when it comes to identifying a particular variety that best suits.

Buckwheat

As a short-term measure, buckwheat could be useful as it grows rapidly in sunny, south-facing places. It has the potential to grow up to a metre in height in the space of just 12 weeks, but is likely to collapse after the first heavy frost – even then, the seed will still prove to be a useful feed source. Perhaps the best use of buckwheat is when incorporated into other mixtures (see 'Mixtures' below).

Kale

Personally, I'm not a huge fan of kale when it is planted on its own as a game crop. It is my experience that game birds do not really like its density and overhead canopy (even when double-drilled) and that, when wet, birds get sodden feathers through either running under it or bursting through its unforgiving leaves when attempting to break cover.

127

With the development of winter-hardy varieties, kale is now, however, a fairly universal game cover crop. With dense top growth and a bare floor below, it does, it must be admitted, provide excellent cover for pheasants. In addition, if kale varieties such as hybrid Colea or Thousand-head are grown and allowed to flower and seed in their second year, they will provide a useful crop of seeds that hold well and don't shed. (Second-year kale is very attractive to partridges – for a first-year feed source, include other crops such as buckwheat, forage rape or millet.)

Club-root in brassicas

Kale is a brassica plant and any type of brassica is likely to suffer from club-root. Wherever possible, such crops should be rotated – perhaps a cover crop could be planted 50/50 with kale and maize, and the two crops alternated from year to year. Rotation will help cut down on the possibility of club-root (particularly on acidic ground), as will regular liming of the land and the planting of club-root resistant seed varieties.

Healthy kale growing well on high land (photo courtesy of Richard Barnes/Kings Game Cover).

Maize

Rather than a single seed type, it might be worth considering using a blend of varieties that has been selected by the seed house from where you are buying because of its ability to combine early maturity with cobs grown at a low height. It should, in addition, mean that it is less susceptible to extreme cold and so crops can be successfully grown as far north as Yorkshire.

Always drill (not broadcast) maize in wide rows to give the birds good access to the crop whilst also aiding good cob development. You might also like to consider planting an adjacent crop of kale/millet/sorghum which will provide a tasty source of feed for the entire season. If you have a rodent (or badger) problem and don't need the maize for feed, think about using a cob-free variety – late-maturing European varieties do not often form cobs.

If maize is being sown after long-term grass, there is a good chance that wireworm will be present and it is therefore essential to specify an appropriate seed treatment when ordering.

How to spot 'Eyespot'

Maize can, in certain climatic conditions, suffer from 'Eyespot' although it does, to some extent, depend on what variety you decide to grow as some are more tolerant than others. You might notice spotting on the leaves towards the end of summer, beginning of autumn and, if you hold the leaf up to the light, it's possible to detect a yellow halo shape around the spot. Cold, damp conditions make matters worse and in some cases, you might notice the whole of the crop looking as if it has been touched by frost.

Experts say that the risk of this spore-borne problem can be lessened in future years by ploughing the game crop areas deep just as soon as the shooting season has finished – and by rotating the crop varieties wherever possible. (On the subject of early ploughing, see 'At the End of the Season' later in this chapter.)

'Poacher' maize growing alongside a cover mix of 'Campaign' – a mix developed to work within the Entry Level Scheme as it is eminently suitable for shooting needs as well as fulfilling the need to provide a natural feed source for wild songbirds (photo courtesy of Richard Barnes/Kings Game Cover).

Millet

Millet is particularly suitable for the southern half of England. The crop is a provider of warmth and some lower level feed when sown with maize. (Millet is frequently seen sown interspersed with maize in alternate 4m drill widths.) Red and white varieties offer different seed maturing times and growth habits. It is also possible to buy Ambush Millet Mix – a combination of white millet and Japanese reed millet. The suppliers claim that reed millet, being a stronger plant and more winter hardy, provides cover while the white millet produces plentiful seed to hold the birds in the cover.

Millet provides useful seeds and is much loved by both pheasants and partridge. To be of optimum value though, it should be planted alongside or as part of another, more robust type of cover crop (photo courtesy of Richard Barnes/Kings Game Cover).

Miscanthus

Miscanthus seems to be the 'in thing' amongst the keepering and shooting fraternity at the moment. Until relatively recently, it has only ever been seen planted by farmers growing it commercially under contract for use as a biomass energy crop. Its success as a cover crop is, however, of great interest and this is as good a time as any to give the crop some consideration. It can reach up to 3 m in height and perhaps its greatest advantage is that, if it is topped off at the end of each shooting season, it will produce new growth annually for at least 10 years – making the initial expense of planting pale in comparison with the annual expenditure involved in planting and caring for more traditional varieties.

Mixtures

There are many types of cover/game crop mixtures on the market, several of which have delightful-sounding names such as Dawn Chorus, Autumn Fettle, Sunny Daze and Campaign Mix!

Typically, mixtures might include a combination of suitable short-stemmed kale varieties, maize, buckwheat, quinoa, sunflowers and phacelia. It is also possible to plant late varieties in the late summer in order to provide a little winter feed and some natural areas attractive to young game bird chicks the following spring. Varieties here might well include winter wheat, triticale, winter linseed, birdsfoot trefoil, fodder radish and mustard.

Beware of potentially 'invasive' species

Care must be taken in your choice of cover crop if you do not wish to incur the wrath of conservationists. As we have seen with the introduction of Japanese knotweed, for instance, some plants not indigenous to the UK have had a detrimental effect on the environment and some 'new' potential cover crops may yet prove to be invasive.

At an international meeting held in Bonn, it was stated that countries should avoid planting crops for biomass fuels that stand a high risk of becoming an invasive species. A subsequent report: 'Biofuel Crops and Non Native Species: Mitigating the Risks of Invasion', worried that many of the plant species being considered for biomass fuels have the potential to become invasive if introduced to new areas.

Here a protective belt of miscanthus forms a natural windbreak around a crop of maize: whereas the maize will weaken and collapse as the shooting season and cold, inclement weather take its toll, the miscanthus will continue to provide cover throughout the winter – and needs little in the way of maintenance.

Some mixtures, such as Campaign Mix, have been developed to work within the Entry Level Scheme and are suitable both for those with an interest in shooting and to fulfill the need to provide a natural feed source for wild songbirds. Suitable for sowing in many regions, it is a useful break crop where kale has been grown over a long period of time and the ground has suffered as a result.

Phacelia

Phacelia is an attractive purple flowering annual that is particularly appealing to insects and might therefore be well worth considering if you are intending to concentrate on early season partridges. It grows to heights of around 60cm and is perhaps ideally sown in annual mixtures – it is, though, very useful (along with mustard) as a green 'fertiliser' that can be ploughed in to enhance existing soil conditions and nutrients.

Phacelia can be planted as late as August if necessary and has the capability of providing quick, thick, dense cover which blankets weeds. If it is too dense though, it will be less attractive to game and certainly difficult to drive during the shooting season. When sowing with other crops it is important to take care with seed rates as it can grow vigorously at the expense of other components. Although phacelia is an annual plant, it self seeds exceptionally well, which might be very useful in certain situations.

Quinoa

In the opinion of many, quinoa is an invaluable game crop option as it provides an abundance of seed and is particularly useful in areas where maize is unviable and 'kale-sickness' is a problem. Quinoa is capable of producing a plentiful amount of seed and therefore is a popular choice of crop for holding partridges and pheasants. Many species of seed-eating songbirds are also attracted to the crop. Commonly grown with kale, quinoa provides cover and feed until it begins to collapse in the first frosts, when kale will continue to provide more permanent cover.

Sorghum

Sorghum is maize-like but slightly shorter in the stem. Dwarf sorghum is, surprise, surprise, even shorter still! Both are useful as a windbreak around other game cover crops and do best in warm, sunny growing conditions so, like maize, are more suited for the southern regions of Britain. Unlike maize, the taller variety is a very slow establishing plant and does not begin to flourish until late July. Conversely, dwarf sorghum, being a single-cross hybrid, is early to mature, and has a good chance of over-wintering without too much weather damage.

Sunflower

This undoubtedly colourful crop is best suited to the southern counties and offers some cover until late September, as well as being a source of tasty seeds for a short period of time. Ideally it should be sown alongside another type of crop or game mixture in order to give cover that lasts, if not right throughout the season, at least up until Christmas and the New Year.

Sunflowers are of some benefit to more sheltered shooting areas but cannot be relied upon to provide any sort of cover once the first frosts occur.

Triticale
A wheat/rye hybrid cereal providing good cover and feed in marginal, low fertility areas (such as acid soils) where it will thrive with little input, triticale offers quick establishment with a relatively short straw length and prolific seed production. In addition to the fact that it grows well on poor or infertile soils, it is winter hardy and has good disease resistance, and is also considered to be one of the few crops that will withstand rabbit and hare damage.

Growing a Permanent Cover Crop

Traditionally, game crops consist of maize, kale, millet, or a melange of seeds sold specifically as being suitable for game. They are all good and have, over the years, proven to be very successful indeed. The only problem is with any of these annual cover crops is that they are just that – annual – and require a great deal of maintenance every spring and early summer.

They are not cheap either and by the time seed, fertilisers, sprays and the services of an agricultural contractor have all been factored into the equation, quite a lot of the shoot's annual budget may have been spent. It is, therefore, worth considering permanent game cover which, once established, more or less looks after itself.

How to grow one

Start in the first year by planting up half the game cover area with a traditional (annual) crop and the other half with one of the perennial type (such as miscanthus). If all goes well, you should be able to replace the traditional side with a planting of perennials in the following year so that by the time the next-but-one shooting season is upon you, you are shooting from a new and permanent crop.

Some possible plant varieties

As well as miscanthus, reed canary grass is useful for particularly exposed places, whilst perennial chicory is ideal for dry conditions with a poor soil structure. Pampas grass has apparently been used on several shoots with great success but there is the slight disadvantage in that it needs to be planted as an individual plant after being grown on in pots and, unless grown in amongst traditional game crops such as millet and/or maize for the first season, is unlikely to give much cover for the first year.

Providing a wind-break

If it looks as though a game crop may become permanent, it will benefit from having a hedge, or at least a few rows of more substantial shrubs and robust grasses included. When doing so, make sure that they will not make access and turning more difficult for a tractor and any attached implements.

I know of one particular shoot that has had considerable success in rolling out mulching strip – the stuff that allows rain water to seep through but prevents weeds from growing – and cutting slits just open enough to plant cuttings of *Lonicera nitida* and Christmas tree saplings in them. The Lonicera provides a bit of warmth and shelter and has the added advantage of being disliked by rabbits and deer, and when the Christmas trees reached the height of about 1.5m, they had the tops cut out of them, which seems to have ensured that the lower branches remain thick and bushy.

Using round bales as a 'hedge'

Where they are plentiful, it could be worth suggesting to the farmer responsible that he stores his large round straw and hay bales alongside the edges of the game crop that are most open to the elements. Even if he needs to use some of them during the shooting season they will have offered some protection for a portion of the autumn and, provided he is not accompanied by any farm dogs, a brief visit by a tractor in order to pick up a few for use in the farm will not disturb any game in the crop. It is not, however, advisable to permit such activity on the morning of the shoot itself!

Planting and Looking After a Game Crop

Before planting, have your soil analysed: analysis of pH and nutrient levels is vital at the outset and should then be carried out every three to four years to ensure that the levels of phosphate, potash, calcium, magnesium and essential trace elements are all as they should be. In a nutshell, pH is for nutrient availability, nitrogen for growth, phosphate for rooting, potash for plant health and calcium for is for plant strength.

Preparation and drilling

A well prepared seedbed is essential for crop health and development, as a rapidly growing game cover has more chance of resisting pest attack. Generally, ploughing and rapid consolidation to conserve moisture is the ideal start for these crops but it is important not to rush the job – ensure that the seed bed is fine and firm as this will help germination and reduce the risk of slug activity. Depending on the advice of your agronomist, spraying off with glyphosate may also be necessary.

> **Timing is crucial**
>
> Many people rush to plant their game crops, but it is well worth waiting until the soil has warmed up sufficiently enough for crops such as maize. The important thing is to have the right seedbed preparation and advice from an agronomist is vital.

Wherever possible, drill rather than broadcast your cover crops. Drilling makes it easier to be certain that the seed is planted at the correct depth and row-width and will provide maximum seed to soil contact, thus enabling speedy germination and plant establishment. Sowing at the correct row width will also improve bird holding and driving capability.

Time spent with an agronomist and your local seed merchant is never wasted – even when a cover crop is established, advice sought and taken regarding ongoing spraying and fertiliser programmes can be the difference between success and failure (photo courtesy of Richard Barnes/Kings Game Cover).

Protection from deer, rabbits and pigeons

Game crops may also require intermediate protection from deer, rabbits and pigeons until they become established. Flexinet rabbit netting which works from an electric fencing unit will help in deterring rabbits and hares. There are also sprays and repellents that can be used (with varying degrees of success) to protect game crops from rabbit, pigeon and deer damage. One such product is a trace element based spray which its north of England manufacturers and suppliers claim is safe to wildlife and the environment and is best applied to young plants while the crop is actively growing. Spraying the headlands is generally judged sufficient against rabbits and deer, but where pigeons are the main problem it is possible to spot-treat weaker areas most at risk.

Other methods of protecting cover crops from the ravages of pigeons include the siting of an artificial hawk that moves in the wind, or kites that make pigeons think a bird of prey is hovering.

Beware of using gas-operated bird scarers indiscriminately: those which are not correctly programmed and set on timers will undoubtedly upset and antagonise the neighbours. It is always best not to provide non-shooting local residents with reasons to complain. The National Farmers' Union (NFU) has guidelines and a code of practice regarding the use of gas-operated bangers.

If you have a deer problem, consider planting sorghum round the edge of the cover crops as they (and rabbits) don't like it. (It is, however, important to remember that it can be poisonous to cloven-hoofed farm livestock.)

Weed control

One disadvantage of relying on farmyard manure to organically supply much of the soil and plants' necessary nutrients is that it is also likely to produce more weeds. The advantages do, however, generally outweigh the disadvantages.

A cover crop planted correctly and managed well can give nearly 100 percent weed control while it is growing. However, a cover crop poorly managed can become a weedy mess and make a huge deposit into the weed seed bank for future years. Following are some tips for avoiding the pitfalls and maximising your chances for success:

• Check the soil nutrients and pH are correct for the type of crop being planted – feed or lime if required.

• Prepare a good weed-free seedbed.

• Plant at the right time: be sure that thousands of weed seeds are not germinating just below the surface when you plant the cover crop. The final shallow tillage to finish the seedbed should take place minutes or hours – not days – before planting. (Planting into an apparently clean seedbed prepared two to five days earlier can result in a weedy cover crop.)

• Use high-quality seed.

• Use optimum seed rates – don't try to scrimp and save on the amount of seed used.

• Crop rotation is essential where weeds have become a persistent problem; doing so will also help reduce soil-borne disease such as club-root in kale and increase soil fertility and structure due to the fact that each subsequent crop will benefit the soil in different ways.

• In a dry spring/early summer, the effect of some herbicides on crops will cause stress to the growing plant. Consider the situation carefully before deciding whether or not to use any.

The stale bed technique

The stale seedbed technique is a well proven weed control system and allows early control of weeds. The technique involves spraying, ploughing and cultivating to encourage weed seeds to germinate in a first flush, then re-spraying; this can help achieve a clean seedbed. This technique is very useful where mixtures are grown and no herbicide can be recommended.

Seed, Ferts and Sprays

The above abbreviation appears on many a shoot budget appertaining to game crops!

Seeds

Seed rates vary tremendously depending on the type of crop being grown: some kale varieties, for example, should be sown at a ratio of 2kg per 0.5ha (in 50cm rows),

A well planted cover crop of the right type (here showing third-year miscanthus) can be self-regulating when it comes to suppressing weed growth.

whilst game mixtures may require 4.5–10kg of seed for the same area. Seed is often supplied in bags, the weight of which indicates the likely ratio: that is, a bag weighing 10kg might well contain seed that needs to be planted at the rate of 10kg per 0.5ha.

As to the question of treated seed: seed treatment is recommended where there is a history of pest problems. Brassicas such as kale can be susceptible to attack by pests such as flea beetle, which can decimate crops if infestation takes place in the first six weeks. Using the seed treatment Ultrastrike not only protects kale against flea beetle, but also provides effective aphid control.

Fertilisers

Use farmyard manure wherever possible – especially on set-aside land. As a farmer, if you are claiming any sort of grant, it is as well to check what fertilisers can or cannot be used – game crops grown as mixtures are viewed as a non-food crop and are subsequently subject to certain conditions and management restrictions.

The issue is complicated: game mixtures, such as kale, quinoa and triticale, grown on un-cropped land, can be classified as green cover but the rules state that no fertiliser should be applied to these covers. If, however, you sow a single game cover strip, the restrictions on herbicide use and cultivations appear not to exist but you are not permitted to use either organic manures or fertilisers to encourage the growth of the game cover strip.

There does, however, appear to be a solution to the fertiliser problem and it is possible to apply for a derogation from the Rural Payments Agency. The request should state the reasons for applying for a derogation, for example for the effective establishment of the green cover, and it should provide full details of the action to be taken as well as explaining the reasons.

Finally, a few perennial crops, such as miscanthus, will become 'self-sufficient' in time; in fact, after the second year, no chemical sprays or fertilisers are required. (The plant naturally dies back in the winter months and all the nutrients from the plant will return into the rhizome complex that will feed the crop for the coming season.)

Fertilisers in drought conditions

According to Hurrells (www.hmseeds.co.uk), at times when '...drought and unpredictable temperatures are taking their toll, crops that have fertiliser placed under the seeds at planting will show an increase in growth and maintain an even plant colour in the difficult weeks of establishment'. Also, 'game crops that are treated with foliar feeds from the start will have a better chance of responding to difficult conditions; such feeds allow the crops to recover faster and grow well'.

Sprays

Chemical sprays should be used as sparingly as possible – especially in situations where the question of organic versus artificial might be an issue. Organic farming uses fertilisers and pesticides but excludes or strictly limits the use of manufactured (synthetic) fertilisers and pesticides (which include herbicides, insecticides and fungicides).

For weed control, a post-emergence bromoxynil x prosulfuron mix such as 'Jester' might be recommended, but it is important to check with your agronomist or seed supplier as, depending on what is being grown, some chemicals just cannot be used without detriment to the plant. For example, you shouldn't use a graminicide on sorghum or millet and, if you are likely to need to spray maize, you must make sure that the maize variety is 'Titus' tolerant so that a chemical such as rimsulfuron can be used.

Particularly when it comes to the subject of crops likely to be of benefit to partridges, it is important that you should only use pesticides as a last resort – and try to avoid using broad-spectrum insecticides after 15 March as these also kill off beneficial insects and spiders that move into the crops in the spring. The loss of this food source is particularly damaging to grey partridges.

Game-friendly alternatives to pesticides

It is accepted that destructive pests could become more prevalent due to global warming and the loss over recent decades of habitat that encourages friendly insects. However, using pesticides to control these pests has a negative environmental impact on biodiversity, and increasingly, organisations such as the GWCT are looking at ways of reducing the use of chemicals to control crop pests by utilising the services of beneficial insects such as beetles, spiders and hoverflies – a process known as biocontrol. Their research and field studies are intended to determine how much land needs to be devoted to habitat that encourages environmentally-friendly insects, such as beetle banks, conservation headlands, wildflower margins and grassy field banks.

At the End of the Season

One of the first jobs once the shooting season has finished is often to 'top' existing game crops in readiness for a coating of farmyard manure prior to being ploughed in the spring. Topping your game crops at this time of year is not necessarily a good idea as retaining some permanent cover is vital over the next couple of months when natural vegetation is at its lowest. The traditional, but unfortunate, destruction of game crops in February can leave game with very little in the way of food and cover, especially if the shoot concerned is one of those that doesn't continue with a regular feeding programme once the shooting season has finished.

Unfortunately, leaving annual crops until the last possible minute before cultivating and planting can cause problems should the weather be wet and cold, or the person responsible for their planting is busy with other, possibly far more lucrative, farming operations.

Dung, farmyard manure, FYM – call it what you will – is a brilliant natural fertiliser adding vital nutrients and 'body' to the soil. Here, well rotted manure lies piled up ready and waiting to be spread on the old cover crop in the spring.

The importance of farmyard manure (FYM)

Game crops are traditionally best placed on high ground and high ground generally has the worst soil – the best of it having eroded over the years, and so a good covering of FYM will add nutrients and structure to the ground once it has been ploughed in. Unfortunately many shoots fail to realise the importance of adding manure until a crop fails – by which time it is too late to do anything for that particular season.

You might have to buy in manure, but it shouldn't cost you much as most farms and livery stables will be only too pleased to be rid of their surplus for not much more than the labour costs involved in collecting, and transportation. All that is then required is for your friendly neighbourhood farmer to spread it for you or, if you normally have your cover crops planted and cared for by a contractor, to factor in his costs for doing so.

CHAPTER 11

━━━━

Shooting Days and Preparation

I always like the buzz of a first day when old friends and acquaintances get together once more after the close season break. There is generally much hand-shaking and many comments as to who looks well and who looks older.

Making People Welcome

Once the shoot helpers and Guns arrive on the morning of the shoot, they will expect to be greeted by someone with an air of confidence and a warm welcome rather than being left hanging about their vehicle, unsure of what to do next.

Throughout the day they should be left with no doubt as to what is happening – in fact, it should all have been explained before setting off from the meeting point. Always try and explain everything to each individual and make them feel that they are the most important person in the world. In the hospitality industry, this undeniable skill is apparently known as 'intangible service' and is highly prized!

Risk Assessments

Should a shoot issue a written list of do's and don'ts at the beginning of each day? As far as the beaters are concerned, I don't personally think that it's necessary. However, to comply with modern day thinking as regards health and safety and risk assessments, the shoot must have previously completed the latter document and made each beater and shoot helper sign a paper to say that they have read and understood it.

The Guns should be treated in the same way and, in addition, must obviously be given a pre-shoot pep talk about what is and what is not allowed to be shot; whether a whistle will signal the start of a drive and that there must be no shooting at all once the whistle or horn has been blown for the end of the drive. This talk is normally done when the Guns are drawing for their peg numbers.

How to draw for numbers

At the beginning of each day, the Guns usually draw a number to decide on the gun peg they will stand at. It is possible to buy any variety of specially-made position finders but a great many shoots make do by pulling out the ace to number eight (or nine) from a suit of playing cards and using those.

On a driven shoot, most Guns move up two pegs on each drive – therefore, if you draw number 'one' for the first drive, you will be standing on peg 'three' for the second, peg 'five' for the third and so on throughout the day. It's an excellent and very fair way of ensuring that each Gun has the chance of being at the centre of the shooting at least a couple of times during the day.

Most shoots indicate where the Guns should stand by means of a number stuck in the cleft of a straight hazel stick: more and more, however, are using short white pegs such as the one illustrated here, which are far less likely to be blown over or knocked by livestock. In addition they look much smarter ... and those with an unruly dog can use them to secure a lead!

Beaters and Other Important People!

One thing that remains the same whether you are a gamekeeper, Gun or casual shoot helper is the camaraderie amongst shooting people: even those who have never met each other before that morning will, by lunchtime, be laughing and joking as if they were life-long friends. This camaraderie is perhaps most apparent in the beating line, especially if it is one where a regular team has been created over a few seasons. Not only does it make the gamekeeper's job a lot easier when everyone knows what is going on and each have their allocated duties, but it also makes being a part of the beating line a great deal more fun.

Beaters and beating

Of course it's all very well for a bit of harmless banter between the drives and at lunchtime, but once the shooting starts, everyone should realise that there's a job to be done. On the big shoots that employ a full-time keeper, his employment depends on a good team of beaters and whilst it might be a day out for the beaters, to him it's one of only a few opportunities to show his employer and his guests what he has been doing in the months prior to the shooting season.

It is every gamekeeper's nightmare to be presented with a team of the guest Guns' children and a request that 'they'd like to come beating for the morning'. Whilst it is undoubtedly a good way of getting them to learn what goes on behind the scenes and should, in theory, be encouraged, in practice, however, sometimes they are just too young and cannot manage to walk in line through a particularly thick piece of game crop – necessitating a kind adult beater picking them up and carrying them through to the end of the drive.

Some beating tips
- Any new member of the team should have the drive explained to them and be placed next to experienced beaters who will point them in the right direction and keep them in line.

- On every shoot, the beating becomes more difficult as the season progresses: birds are getting fewer in number and those still around are more wary of disturbance. Whereas earlier in the season, it might not have mattered if a few ran out of a game crop or down a hedgerow, it does now and any beaters delegated as 'stops' must keep a careful look-out for pheasants creeping forward in order to work out a possible escape route. Just one person walking quietly up and down in view of, but not close to, the cover to be driven can make the difference between success and failure.

- The deployment of 'stops' is an essential part of a successful shooting day and it will definitely pay to spend more time either 'stopping-off' likely escape routes or in detailing small groups of beaters to bring in hedgerows back to the proposed drives. There might only be half a dozen birds up each hedge, but their absence in a particular beat may make a lot of difference by the end of the day.

A young keeper and his crew of beaters during a break between drives. As can be seen from this photo, beaters can be young or old, male or female – dogs don't necessarily have to be gundogs either!

Flaggers and flankers

Flags are a very important part of a partridge drive: even if the beaters do not carry them in the manner of drivers on a grouse moor, there should be at least a couple of flankers carrying flags at each end of the line, as these can often be successful in turning errant birds towards the Guns. Flanking is something of a skilled job and should only be given to shoot helpers experienced enough to understand a little of the likely movements of partridges.

The art of flanking and flagging

• Keeping the flag high in the air and waving it constantly tends to lose impact and it is far better to carry the flag to one side of the body and only raise it at the last moment. A few quick flicks, especially if the flag is one that 'cracks' as it is waved, will be much more likely to have the desired effect.

• Traditionally, all partridge beaters would have carried flags, but as it is more likely that partridges will only be a diversion on a shoot that relies predominantly on pheasants, it is probably sufficient for just the beaters at each end of the line to be equipped with them.

• Custom-made flags are cheap to buy and fit easily into a jacket pocket, so it is not a bad idea to purchase a dozen or so and issue them to some of the regular members of the team. Failing that, make your own from fertiliser or feed bags and keep them in the beaters' transport so that, when driving game crops and areas where partridges are likely to be encountered, it is a simple matter for a few of the team to swap their regular sticks for flags.

Flags on a pheasant shoot

Flags and flag-men are not necessary on a pheasant shoot. You sometimes see them positioned between the Gun line and the end of the drive but they look wrong and most experienced shooting people do not like to see them. Flags will not turn pheasants – they might make them fly a little higher as they come out of the drive, but having flag-men there in the first place suggests that you already know your birds are not likely to prove to be of high, sporting quality. It is far better to flush pheasants further back in the cover, or to consider revamping the drive entirely.

Pickers-up and picking up

Whether professional or amateur, family member or stranger, the mechanics and skills of being an effective picker-up remain the same. The objective is, put simply, to retrieve all shot game and ensure that it finds its way to the game cart and from there to the larder.

• Unlike perfect children who should be seen and not heard, perfect pickers-up should, in the opinion of many experienced Guns and keepers, be neither seen nor heard – at least not until the end of the day.

• To do their work efficiently, pickers-up need to be positioned perhaps 300 yards behind the Guns whilst the drive is going on and then, once the keeper's whistle to denote the end of the drive has been blown, work slowly forward before giving the Gun line a final sweep – by which time, the Guns and beaters will be well on their way to the next drive.

• It might be prudent to leave one picker-up in the vicinity of the Guns in order to be able to act on specific information regarding the whereabouts of any unfound game.

• Ideally, the picking-up team will be led by a designated captain who knows the ground and is familiar with all the drives.

Pickers-up and their dogs are essential when it comes to collecting shot game from inaccessible places. A dog that is bold in cover and retrieves well from water is a god-send.

Prevent Undue Noise by Limiting Vehicles

Contrary to what those of us who have reared and worked with them for several years might, on occasions, think, game birds are not stupid and they still have a great degree of the self-preservation instinct left in their breeding – which is exactly as it should be.

Guns can often be their own worst enemy and fail to realise that it is difficult enough driving birds over the line without the extra trials and tribulations brought about by unnecessary noise. To my mind, one of the best ways of preventing too much is to limit the amount of vehicles used on the shoot.

It is becoming increasingly common for the pickers-up team to use their own vehicles. Their wish to do so is quite understandable but they and the Guns must be given strict instructions as to where and when they can park – it would not be the first time that a row of Guns or pickers-up vehicles have turned birds back over the heads of beaters blanking in a piece of ground. The beaters are not generally a problem as they are likely to have been transported from drive to drive in a communal trailer.

Avoiding Accidents Travelling Around the Shoot

There have, sadly, been some serious accidents that occurred when beaters and other shoot helpers were travelling around the estate on tractors and trailers. With this in mind, the BASC have a Code of Practice on the subject, the full contents of which can be viewed by visiting:
www.basc.org.uk/en/codes-of-practice/transport-of-beaters.cfm Briefly though, its main content is as follows:

• Trailers should be in sound road-worthy condition.

• There should be enough safe and secure seating for all.

• All passengers must remain seated whilst the trailer is moving.

• Open trailers must have a guard-rail between 920mm and 1,050mm above floor level (an intermediate-rail and toe-rail are advisable).

• A safe means of access such as secure steps should be included – and a solid hand-rail provided.

• The driver should be experienced in towing a trailer and drive carefully with consideration for all passengers at all times.

• Lights might need to be considered – especially red tail-lights. Also, slow-moving vehicles with a legislated maximum speed of 25mph must be fixed with an amber warning beacon.

Beaters' trailers (and indeed, any form of shoot transport) should be well maintained and conform to road traffic regulations.

Positioning Partridge Pegs

Traditionalists say that, in the interests of safety, a set of hides or pegs positioned specifically for partridges should be in a perfectly straight line. This should, perhaps be the ideal, but there may well be cases, such as a gap in the tree-line at the corner of a field, where an end Gun would be more successful if he or she were placed slightly forward of the main line. To a team of experienced and competent Guns, this will cause no problems, but if there is any doubt about the safety aspect, follow the traditionalist's advice and keep the Gun line straight.

Non-Toxic Shot

Way back in 1999, restrictions on the use of lead shot were brought into force in England under The Environmental Protection Regulations. There are three main situations where the use of lead shot is illegal.

1. For all shooting on or over the foreshore (the area below the high water mark of ordinary spring tides).

2. For all shooting on or over Sites of Special Scientific Interest that have been designated by the government.

3. To shoot any duck, goose, coot, moorhen, snipe or golden plover.

Although the 1999 legislation initially only concerned England, the Welsh Assembly introduced similar restrictions in 2002 and Scotland in March 2005, but it took until 2009 before similar legislation occurred in Northern Ireland. The law applies to all wetlands including foreshore areas. Inland flight ponds, no matter how small, are counted as wetland features, as are fields which frequently flood or which include streams or ponds.

Tungsten – good or bad for the environment?

One of the alternatives to lead shot is made from tungsten and there are some schools of thought that suggest the use of lead is far less damaging. In the summer of 2011, the Union of Country Sports Workers was asking country sports' supporters to sign a petition against an even wider lead shot ban and asking the Secretary of State for DEFRA to seriously consider removing the lead shot ban for wildfowling. Their press release said: 'Tungsten ammunition is no longer used in some parts of the world ... due to health risks from the so-called "green" non-toxic ammunition. We are asking if ... using tungsten-based shot is a health risk to wildlife and the environment.'

In some situations and locations (such as on Sites of Special Scientific Interest), lead shot cartridges are not permissible and only the non-toxic type may be used (photo courtesy of Elliot Hobson).

Hard Weather Bans for Wildfowl

During periods of exceptionally severe weather the Secretary of State for the Environment and the Secretary of State for Scotland may impose a ban on the shooting of wildfowl and certain other birds. Notice of such a ban is given in selected national newspapers and is broadcast by radio stations. The BASC always attempts to give advance warning of a hard weather ban to affiliated wildfowling clubs.

How is a decision arrived at?

The shooting of wildfowl and waders is normally suspended after 14 consecutive days of freezing weather. The criteria for triggering the severe weather procedures are based on the air and grass temperatures collected daily by 25 coastal weather stations around Britain. The procedure is as follows:

- If more than half of the weather stations have recorded a minimum of seven consecutive days of frozen ground in Scotland or England/Wales or both, the Joint Nature Conservation Committee and/or Scottish Government informs BASC accordingly.

- The information from each weather station is gathered each morning and reflects the lowest air and grass temperature recorded that night. This combination of minimum temperatures indicates the likelihood of difficult feeding conditions for feeding waterfowl.

- If the severe weather looks set to continue BASC informs its members generally but particularly the secretaries of its wildfowling and game shooting clubs, joint councils, syndicates and gamekeepers that, if the weather conditions continue for a further six days, then a protection order suspending the shooting of wildfowl and waders in the appropriate country is likely to be signed on the 13th day, to take effect at 00.01am on the 15th day.

- A voluntary restraint may be called for before the imposition of one which is legally enforced.

The Likely Effects of General Weather Conditions

Irrespective of the effects that hard weather may have on wildfowl and waders, general weather conditions can sometimes affect the success or otherwise of both moorland and low-ground game shooting. Personal experience has led me to deduce the following:

- Mild sunny days are, not, as a rule, the best for shooting and when the weather is such, unless you send a few beaters to blank in any surrounding hedgerows and streams towards a main drive, you can lose quite a few pheasants due to their propensity to wander into odd corners during such weather conditions.

- Another disadvantage of a sunny day is the fact that the birds either cannot see the line of Guns and fly low, or the Guns cannot see the birds.

- In mild 'muggy' weather, personal experience tells me that game birds are less inclined to fly – like the rest of us, they obviously feel more lethargic.

- Heavy rain overnight, but which stops at breakfast-time and results in a dull morning, is the gamekeeper's dream; heavy rain throughout the day, however, only results in sodden birds, especially if they are being driven through wet cover crops and their flight feathers become saturated.

- Wind is an interesting one. A pilot of my acquaintance tells me that you should never take off with the wind in either a helicopter or light aircraft, as it becomes very difficult to get airborne. Putting the same theory into practice regarding pheasants or partridge, one should, perhaps, try and ensure that the 'beats' are driven into the wind, but if you do, will the birds achieve an upward lift as a plane

Heavy rain throughout the day results in sodden birds (and some wet beaters!), especially if they are being driven through wet cover crops and their flight feathers become saturated (photo courtesy of Elliot Hobson).

would, or will they merely be forced off-course and, though no choice of their own, veer away from the waiting Gun line?

• In theory, fog should detrimentally affect a pheasant or partridge shoot but in practice, some of the best and most difficult birds that I have ever seen have been as a result of what can only be described as a 'hovering' pheasant hanging high over a steep valley – where the disoriented bird will eventually land is, it must be admitted, a very real worry to the keeper, but to the Guns, such unusual tactics make for an unusually testing shot.

Hanging Game

Large sporting estates have always had a game larder – architecturally, they were often ornate and quite splendid affairs. To conform to 2006 food hygiene regulations, you might need to store your game in a chilled unit prior to its collection by the game dealer. (You might also need to have completed a game-handling course – for more information on which, see Chapter 1.)

At the risk of 'teaching grandmother to suck eggs' and possibly insulting the intelligence of experienced gamekeepers reading this, traditionally, game birds are hung by their heads whilst rabbits, hares and the carcasses of boar or venison are hung by their back legs, heads facing downwards.

Hares are unusual in that they are normally hung with their guts still intact, whereas rabbits and deer have their intestines removed as soon as possible after being killed.

Wild duck are not generally hung as, for some reason, the practice does not seem to improve their flavour, but if you have a particular yearning to do so, they, unlike pheasants and partridge, are normally hung by their feet. Pigeons are also usually dressed 'fresh' and do not require hanging.

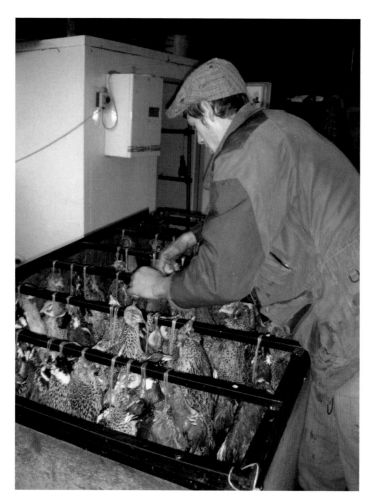

As soon as is practicable, shot game should be taken from the game cart and placed in a chiller (here seen to the back left of the trailer) prior to collection by the game dealer.

Where shot birds go

It has long been thought that most of the birds shot on UK estates which are collected by game dealers eventually find their way into Europe (often via France). The figures are, however, not as high as was once the case. An article in *The Field* in late 2010 indicated that whereas in 1999, the 'game meat and offal' sales exported from Britain to France was around 860 tonnes and was valued at £2.3 million, less than one decade later the tonnage exported had dropped to 532 tonnes.

Hopefully the reason for the decline is due to the fact that more and more people in the UK are becoming accustomed to the taste of game. Logistics must, however, play some part. Game that is exported to France from British shoots generally involves a process using metal tags, individually marked sealed boxes, health officer inspections and, of course, plenty of paperwork and form-filling.

Hanging game for home use

Generally, hanging game for a few days will undoubtedly increase the flavour and tenderise the meat. Just how long you hang it depends on how 'gamey' you like your meat to taste, what type of game you're hanging (a grouse, for instance, will taste much stronger after being hung for three days than will a pheasant or partridge given the same amount of time) and the weather conditions (thundery weather can turn a bird rapidly, even if the temperature is not high).

In warm weather, two or three days might be all that is required, but, during an exceptionally cold period, a week or even up to ten days would not be too long.

Keeper's and Beaters' Days

At the end of each season, it has long been traditional that the last few shooting days have been given over to tenants' and farmers' shoots, and keeper's and beaters' days – the idea being to thank all who have helped throughout the year. Times change, however, and it is nowadays more likely that the modern shoot has not only a limited number of estate tenants to pacify, but also the very major financial consideration that some of these birds traditionally offered to the shoot helpers

Shot game can very quickly deteriorate in unseasonally warm weather – or during the first autumnal days of the shooting season. Find a cool place to hang your game: try draping them with muslin and securing with rubber bands in order to protect against flies.

could be sold as a means of gaining extra shooting revenue. One day that remains as strong and as necessary as it ever was is the keeper's, or beaters' day.

Stay safe

The annual beaters' day is eagerly looked forward to by almost all of the shoot helpers and is, for many, the only opportunity they have to shoot at game. Great care must, however, be taken that no rules are being broken and that any necessary legal requirements are complied with.

There is no reason why the more inexperienced should not join in the fun, but it is essential that someone well versed in shooting etiquette and gun safety is standing with them at all times. Although none of us likes the sometimes extreme and ridiculous measures involved with risk assessments and health and safety, the morning of the beaters' day may, in fact, be one time when some of the more pertinent points should be brought to the attention of the assembled group.

Keeping Game Books and Records

All shoots keep game book records – or at least they should. There are many reasons why records can prove useful: the most obvious being to show seasonal bag averages which will undoubtedly be of value when a season's shooting is being let to a syndicate or even, sadly, when an estate has to be put on the market. Admittedly, this is more important on a grouse moor where a ten-year bag average may need to be assessed, but, although the numbers of pheasants and partridge on a low-ground shoot can be predicted to a degree by the amount of birds released, long-term records are, however, well worth maintaining.

By doing so, one can work out which drives work best at what part of the season, in certain winds or weather conditions and whether beating one particular woodland or game crop in a sequence with another will help or hinder the forthcoming drives. Assuming all other things are equal, there is also the general interest in comparing the amount of birds shot from year to year at any given point throughout the season.

In days gone by it was traditional for most shoots to fill in game cards and either hand them to the Guns at the end of the day or to send them one a couple of days later. On it would be recorded the drives, the numbers shot on each one, a total for the day and the estate's running total for the season so far. The names of fellow guests were often also included. You might like to consider maintaining this very worthwhile tradition.

How to Assess Your Seasonal Returns

No matter how good a gamekeeper you are, the average returns (i.e. birds shot) will be surprisingly low – there are several reasons for this, not least disease, non-acclimatisation when birds are first released, predation and even something as simple as wandering off over the boundary onto the neighbour's land.

Working out your actual return at the end of the season is simple: it's just a question of taking the number of birds released, working out how many have been shot on each shooting day and taking the percentage.

Adding up and making sense of financial returns

The 2010/11 Shoot Benchmarking Survey carried out by land agents Smiths Gore suggests that, taking into consideration variable costs such as fuel, the production of game crops, feed, shoot equipment and the like, and then adding the total of fixed costs (gamekeeper's wages, housing, allowances, rent to outside parties, etc.), gave an average cost per bird put down on the shoot as being £12.28.

The same survey indicates that there was a difference between commercial and non-commercial shoots when it came to returns: the first's national average being 37 percent, the latter's, 42 percent.

Elsewhere, the same survey suggests that on commercial shoots, the price charged to the Guns per bird shot was, on average, around, £30. This leaves an interesting discrepancy between the price charged and the cost per bird released – one which is, however, easily explained by the following simple sum:

Total cost of bird released	£12.28
Divided by return	say, 39 percent
Equals total cost per bird shot	£31.49

'My shooting has cost me *how* much?!!'

CHAPTER 12

The Gamekeeper's Dog

Even in this modern age, there is little or no technology that can replace the gamekeeper's canine companion. The Hunting Act 2004 has made it either illegal or difficult for some of the keeper's traditional duties with his dog (see Chapter 4, 'Predators and Relevant Legislation'), but even so, it would be a poor keeper without at least one animal at his heel.

What Dog?

Terriers very definitely have their place as a keeper's dog, especially when out and about in pursuit of vermin. Gundogs are, though, the type you most commonly think of when considering the typical gamekeeper's companion.

Possible breeds are many and varied: the Victorian or Edwardian keeper would most likely have had a curly-coated or flat-coated retriever by his side, but these are nowadays very much the exception rather than the rule.

Their place has generally been taken by the Labrador or spaniel; there are, however, those gamekeepers with a particular interest in dogs who prefer the uniqueness (and some might say, challenge!) of foreign hunt, point, retrieve (HPR) breeds such as the Braque d'Auvergne, German Pointer, Hungarian Vizsla, Italian Spinone, Large Munsterlander or Weimaraner.

As far as spaniels are concerned, the English Springer was, for many decades, just about the only type you would see in the keeper's kennel and out on the shooting field. They have, arguably, been usurped by the Cocker in recent years, which in turn, have been joined by minority breeds such as the Clumber, Field and Sussex Spaniel.

Pointers and setters (not including those in the list of HPRs) are more specialised and it would be rare to see known British breeds like the English Setter, Gordon Setter, Irish Setter or Pointer working anywhere else but on the grouse moors or wide open partridge 'manors'. Interestingly, in January 2012, the Kennel Club warned that the English Setter, one of Britain's oldest native dog breeds, was at risk of 'extinction' and pointed out that, in 2011, only 234 of them were registered – a 33 percent decline on 2010. Furthermore, there has been a decline of almost two-thirds in the number of English Setters today, compared with ten years ago.

Weimaraner retrieving a canvas dummy from water as part of early training (photo courtesy of Sue Knight).

Dogging-in

Every gamekeeper knows that pheasants like to wander. Dogging-in is just one way of pushing straying pheasants from the boundaries of a shoot back into the middle. The type of dog used is immaterial but it is, in the opinion of many, essential that the keeper should be on his feet rather than, as is so often seen these days, from the seat of a quad bike with a dog sitting in the bucket! Modern technology can be applied to many tasks, but I would suggest that dogging-in is not one of them.

Dogging-in is often neglected as part of the daily routine, but it is to my mind, an important part of successful keepering – and not just when the poults first start leaving the release pens in the late summer. In the late autumn, if time permits, pushing birds back towards the centre of the shoot is also worth considering.

There are at least two reasons for this: first, pheasants might take to roosting in the boundary trees of certain warm, sheltered areas as the weather becomes colder and, second, some of the quiet, normally un-shot scrubby places become an attractive safe haven once shooting begins.

Dogging-in partridges without a dog!

Unlike pheasants, dogging back partridges into the centre of the shoot is often better done without dogs! A person walking down the boundary hedge of a stubble field can do just as much good with some frantic flapping of a flag – either bought from a game suppliers or home made with a shank of hazel, a few felt nails and a plastic fertiliser bag – as they can with a dog (particularly, if the dog happens to be of a slightly unruly nature).

Red-legs are more likely to run before flying, unlike the grey partridge whose first instinct is to fly at the first sign of potential danger. Nevertheless, the 'crack' of a flag will panic a covey of red-legs into flying from the boundary and back towards the point from which they have been released.

Dogs in the Beating Line

Generally a trained and well controlled dog in the beating line is a useful asset. There's a general assumption that a dog simply intended for such use doesn't really need much training, and that dogs that work in such a situation are somehow inferior to those which accompany the pickers-up or Guns – but that assumption is most definitely erroneous. Here are five comments based on personal experience!

1. Working in the beating line with your dog on a lead is totally impractical as it's impossible not to get caught up when going through heavy cover or a tall stand of cover crop such as maize.

2. When working a dog loose, you'll soon discover that it's virtually impossible to stop it from pegging unshot game. Almost all gundog breeds are prone to peg, with spaniels being the worst. Whatever happens, you must never tell it off for bringing you a bird, shot or not – if you do, it will be far less keen to bring you anything the next time.

3. A good beating dog should always hunt close to his or her master, be responsive to the whistle and never be tempted to chase anything, however irresistible it may be.

4. Unless your dog is trained to a very high standard, it's difficult to take it beating one week and picking-up the next – however, unless you can afford a dog for every occasion, this is exactly what you may need to do, so continuous training and control is therefore essential.

5. Watch your dog carefully between drives: quite often, the handler's attention is elsewhere as he or she talks to a fellow beater and there is the excitement of other dogs milling around. In such a situation, a dog can get disorientated, or take advantage of the circumstances in order to prematurely start the next drive. So, unless your dog is without question and, to use an equine term, totally 'bombproof', never feel that it is beneath your dignity, or a sign of a badly trained dog, to keep yours on a lead at such times.

Collars and Docked Tails

Whilst it is legal for your dog to be collarless whilst being used for sporting purposes, The Control of Dogs Order 1992 states that any dog in a public place must wear a collar to which must be attached a disc containing the owner's name, address and postcode.

A micro-chip implanted into the dog's neck by a veterinary surgeon is a good idea and is far more effective than the traditional collar and name tag: in the

Well trained and biddable dogs like these are an asset in the beating line: not only will they flush birds from thick woodland (hopefully in the direction of the standing Guns!) but, after the drive has finished, they can help pick up fallen game. On the other hand, on all but the roughest of 'rough' shoots, an unruly dog is more of a hindrance than a help.

Electric collars as a training aid

Electric shock collars are hugely popular in America and there are already some 500,000 in use in the UK. Some are designed to stop a dog from straying out of a garden whilst others are intended to shock when detonated by the owner pressing a button on a walkie-talkie-like device as a corrective measure whilst training. Manufacturers compare the current to that of a static shock, but animal charities say the technique is cruel and inhumane and claim that dogs can tell whether they have the collar on and behave accordingly. They also fear that owners who use the collars to prevent one type of bad behaviour will be tempted to keep using them to correct other problems, no matter how minor. Electric shock collars were banned by the Welsh Assembly in March 2010, but are still currently (no pun intended) legal in England and Scotland. However, their legality is due to be debated in Parliament at Westminster and in Scotland.

unfortunate event of a dog being stolen, there is a far greater chance of a dog's true ownership being proved.

Legal tail-docking

There is other legislation which, whilst it makes common sense for the pet owner, complicates matters when it appertains to sporting dogs. The Animal Welfare Act 2006 introduced wide-ranging provisions against neglect and cruelty, but the most important for shooting folk relates to tail docking.

In England and Wales (not Scotland, where a complete ban was introduced in April 2007) there is now an official exemption allowing the tails of some sporting breeds (spaniels, hunt/point/retrieve breeds and terriers) to be docked legally by a vet as long as requirements for proof of a working career are met. In Northern Ireland, where legislation similar to that imposed in Scotland was originally decreed, law-makers have now included an exemption for working dogs after animal welfare issues were raised.

If you buy a puppy with a docked tail, make sure that the breeder gives you the necessary official paperwork – normally a certificate signed by their vet.

> ### Tail-docking in Scotland
>
> Immediately prior to the 2011/12 shooting season, a questionnaire was released which sought the opinions of owners of working gundogs and terriers living in Scotland. Brought about by the University of Glasgow's School of Veterinary Medicine's research into the effect the ban has had on working dogs since it was introduced, the information received will be used by lobbyists to persuade the Scottish Parliament to reconsider the matter.

Veterinary Matters

It is in the real emergencies when a good vet comes into their own. Although some of the bigger shoots organise days during the week, it is a pretty safe bet that most field sports are carried out on a Saturday. Normally surgeries are not staffed on these days and so a local contact becomes doubly important. It will pay to carry with you the surgery's 'out-of-hours' number so that immediate steps can be taken in the event of an accident. Such advice might appear pessimistic, but it is better to be prepared before an incident rather than panicking afterwards.

The opinions of individual vets and their governing body, the Royal College of Veterinary Surgeons, have been much sought after in recent years and their comments on such issues as the Hunting Act and tail-docking have been very important in ensuring that the 'pro' hunting and shooting lobby has its say.

Troublesome ticks

Because of the type of cover through which they hunt and work, the gamekeeper's dog is probably more liable to becoming a host to ticks than is the average pet animal.

Spaniels, be they Cockers (on the left) or English Springers, have always been docked due to the fact that their enthusiasm in the densest of cover could quite easily cause a full tail to very quickly become damaged and bleeding. Despite certain government restrictions, veterinary surgeons are still legally permitted to remove a portion of the tail not long after birth.

As is well known, ticks are carriers of several diseases, Lyme disease being the main one. Leaving the head attached might well result in an exchange of blood between tick and host and doing so may just possibly cause a transmission of disease if that particular tick happens to be a carrier; far better to use a 'tick-twister' – which can be bought very cheaply from most pet shops and/or your local vet.

Old wives' tricks might not be the best
Removing ticks by the various old wives' methods is not generally recommended. Although many people swear by the application of petroleum jelly, lighter fluid and the like in the perceived hope that it will cause the tick to either lose its grasp or actually suffocate, it is nowadays thought that such remedies may well cause the tick to disgorge the contents of its stomach directly into the host's bloodstream, thus further increasing the chance of infection.

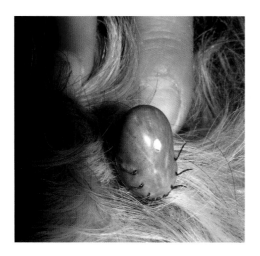

A well fed tick! On short-haired dogs such as Labradors, a tick might be easier to spot than on a flat-coat retriever or spaniel so it is as well to be constantly on the look-out. Take care when removing one and don't be tempted into using some of the 'old wives' tales' that sadly abound: a 'tick twister' available from your vet or pet suppliers might be the best answer (photo courtesy of MH/Veterinary Ltd).

Mites and allergies

Mites are often so small that a veterinarian will require a microscope to make an unmistaken identification. Parasites of any description are the most common source of skin problems in dogs and, due to all the scratching and rubbing that an animal will do in order to relieve itself by itching, many secondary problems may arise.

Allergies are another common cause of skin problems. A dog, like a human, can be allergic to almost anything, but some common causes of allergies in dogs are pollen, dust, mould and grass, with which all working dogs come into regular contact.

Canine skin allergy symptoms include rashes, very itchy skin, scratching constantly, rubbing the muzzle and often chewing on their paws. Others may have ears that feel hot to the touch. It is possible to have your vet conduct an allergy test and once the cause has been identified, it may be practicable to remove it from the dog's everyday life. If, however, the allergy is from things that are uncontrollable such as pollen, grass and mould spores, the veterinarian can arrange to have an 'antigen' made up specifically for the dog. This is almost always administered by injection and can show quite dramatic results.

Treating harvest mite larvae attacks

Harvest mite larvae – which can be recognised as clusters of orange/red dust attached to the dog's hair – can cause severe problems and an unhappy animal. Itching develops in a dog within about half a day of exposure, but the discomfort can continue for several weeks.

Itching can, apparently, be relieved by omega 3 and 6 oils (see also 'Fish oil helps your dog think!' below) and there are several proprietary treatments, including creams and sprays, that help clean up the irritation and encourage the healing process – as well as providing protection from bacterial infection.

Fish oil helps your dog think!

As we have all long known, eating fish is good for the brain. Undeniably good for humans, it is of no less value to working dogs in general and the gamekeeper's dog in particular.

Fish oil helps promote healthy brain development and function, and is ideal for puppies, nursing or pregnant bitches and senior dogs. Pure cod liver oil is good, or it is nowadays possible to purchase salmon oil as a complementary omega-3 supplement containing essential fatty acids which naturally occur in many cold water fish (such as salmon).

It is these essential fatty acids that assist in the healthy structure of nerves and cells and also in brain development. Eicosapentaeonic acid (EPA) is also useful in maintaining healthy joints, circulation, cardiac function, and general all-round health.

Proposed amendments to the Breeding of Dogs Act 1973

At the time of writing, there is talk of the Welsh Assembly amending the Breeding of Dogs Act. If their proposals are successful, it might mean that any gamekeeper or shooting person with three or more breeding bitches needs to register as an official breeder should they be thinking of breeding two or more litters of puppies in any 12-month period. The BASC has made representation to the Assembly proposing that owners of genuine working dog breeds be allowed to produce up to four litters per year before registration is required.

You only have to look at the back of any shooting magazine in order to see modern attractive sectional kennelling for sale. There is, though, a certain charm in housing your working gundogs in beautifully constructed brick-built Victorian kennels – examples of which are still to be found in the stable block of some estates, or attached to traditional gamekeepers' housing (photo courtesy of Sue Knight).

To Kennel or Not to Kennel – That Is the Question!

Should you keep your working dog indoors as part of the family, or should it be kennelled outdoors? It is a subject that has vexed gundog owners and trainers for many a long year. Much does, of course, depend on the breed of dog and the owner's lifestyle, but a few thoughts and ideas might help you decide:

• A commonly held school of thought suggests that a dog under training is better off in a kennel environment because, when out and about with its trainer, it will be focused on its handler. (On the other hand, there are also those who feel that a young dog kept within the family environment will be far better 'humanised'.

• A compromise might be to use a 'cage' as a kennel in the house, which will allow a dog its own secure environment to which it can go to get out of the way of family hustle and bustle. This is an option that wasn't open to keepers of the past as 'cages' are a relatively new idea.

For safety reasons as much as anything else, it is far better to keep working gundogs contained in a travel cage rather than allow them free access to the vehicle luggage area (photo courtesy of Elliot Hobson).

- Alternatively, consider an outdoor kennel for the times you are out of the house, but allow your dog(s) access to your home at times suitable to you.

- An outdoor kennel can also be useful for the times when dogs are brought in muddy and wet after a day's work – although they should, of course, always be towel-dried before being kennelled, putting them in there for an hour or so will prevent much dirt from finding its way into your home.

- However they are constructed, outdoor kennels must be dry and draught-proof, preferably with a raised bed both in the sleeping area and in the run.

- Some manufactured kennels have an option of a covered roof over the outdoor run; they will obviously cost more but are undoubtedly worth considering.

- Outdoor kennels should be 'lockable' – there are plenty of unscrupulous people ready and willing to steal and sell a well-trained, useful dog whether it be gundog or terrier. A security light and sensor are also a good idea.

Field Trials and Working Tests

Many gamekeepers are enthusiastic dog handlers and work their dogs, not only on a shooting day, but also enjoy competing in field trials and working tests – a 'busman's holiday' if you like!

Field trials take place during the shooting season over terrain on which live game can be found and shot whereas working tests simulate a working day and cold game or canvas dummies may be used.

How to enter

Generally, you have to be a member of a gundog club in order to enter; there are probably 170 such organisations in Britain that cater for retrievers, spaniels, the hunt, point, retrieve types (HPRs), plus specific breeds. As far as the main breeds are concerned, there are three main types of trial: Novice, All Aged and Open. If the dog wins a novice it can normally then only enter All Aged or Open and winning an Open Stake is the only way to achieve FTCh status – a very desirable qualification when it comes to proving working ability in a pedigree, especially if you're intending breeding from your dogs.

Obviously what the judges are looking for depends entirely on the type of breed under scrutiny: spaniels are expected to hunt up in search of game between two Guns and retrieve any game shot for them, whereas retrievers will be required to walk quietly in line or behind a Gun until a potential retrieve is shot. All are, however, expected to be well trained and quiet – which would straight away eliminate several dogs of my acquaintance!

Working tests

Gundog working tests are often organised by clubs for their members, but it is sometimes possible to enter without being a member – there are also 'fun' gundog tests and scurries at many of the country fairs held during the summer months. All involve testing the ability of the dogs to work using dummies. Different groups and breeds are tested on different things depending on what their job would be in the field. There are different stakes that can be entered at working tests, including Puppy tests, Novice Dog/Handler and Open tests. Scurries are usually held against the clock and any gundog breed can compete to be the fastest to return with a dummy which it has seen being thrown.

Gamekeepers' Dogs at Crufts

Long before it became associated with show dogs, Crufts was the Mecca for gamekeepers and shooting people; in fact, the now defunct Gamekeepers' Association used to hold their annual general meeting there and it was a place where gamekeepers would sometimes be interviewed prior to changing employment

Entrants at an English Springer spaniel field trial – and a cold looking one at that! Obviously what the judges are looking for depends entirely on the type of breed under scrutiny but, generally, spaniels of any kind are expected to hunt up in search of game between two Guns and then retrieve any game shot (photo courtesy of Sue Knight).

at the end of the season. In amongst it all were held classes for gamekeepers' dogs – a tradition that still, fortunately, survives today under the combined organisational skills of the Kennel Club and BASC.

A bit of history
As the BASC website recounts:

> *The Gamekeepers' Association of the United Kingdom was founded in 1900; a year later Crufts was developed out of the Gamekeepers' Association Annual General Meeting.*
>
> *In 1978, the Gamekeepers' Association became incorporated with the Wildfowlers' Association of Great Britain and Ireland which, in 1982, changed its name to the British Association for Shooting and Conservation.*
>
> *Up to 1989 the running of the Gamekeepers' ring at Crufts was in the hands of some of the old Gamekeepers' Association committee. After the Show in 1989 the old team decided to call it a day and BASC was approached to see if it would be interested in picking up the baton [as a result of which] a number of new sponsors were found to provide some excellent trophies, and two new classes were introduced for retired Gamekeepers and for Regional Teams.*

Showing opportunities today
Today every dog is judged to the breed standard, but major consideration is given to its appearance, looks and conformation as a working gundog which has just finished a hard shooting season. At one time held at the beginning of February,

The Gamekeepers' Class at Crufts in which a dog has to be registered to a gamekeeper but may be shown by another person (photo courtesy of Mark Ridley/TSIPhotography).

since moving to the National Exhibition Centre in Birmingham, Crufts has been held in March, and this has given more keepers from all parts of the country the opportunity to support what was once one of the premier events in the gamekeeper's calendar.

In 2004, a new class was introduced which added opportunity for involvement by not just gamekeepers, but also pickers-up and beaters. Known as the 'BASC Working Gundog Team Competition', each team member has to be verified by a gamekeeper as having very regularly worked on their shoot throughout the season. Three dogs and their handlers make up this team (plus one reserve).

In addition, there are at least three classes that are of particular interest to all gamekeepers and shoot helpers:

1. Gamekeepers – in which a dog has to be registered to a gamekeeper but may be shown by another person

2. Working Gundog Best Dog

3. Working Gundog Best Bitch

NB: All dogs entered into the second and third classes above must have regularly worked during the previous season and this must be qualified by certification by a gamekeeper.

Gamekeepers' Dogs as Film Stars!

Forget the likes of Rin-Tin-Tin (a German Shepherd) or Lassie (a show-type Collie) or, more recently, the Jack Russell terrier that stole the hearts of many when he appeared in the 2011/12 box office hit *The Artist*, and instead think gundogs! Whenever a period piece is required on film or television, a dog of a breed known at the time will be required by the producers and researchers. If an example of the breed is well trained (as hopefully most keepers' dogs are), there's an opportunity to take advantage of such a situation!

For myself, I once was charged with keeping a Cocker Spaniel sitting looking quizzical despite all an actress's efforts to get it to come towards her (a firm out-stretched hand used almost universally as a 'stop' signal as I was standing out of shot did the trick!). In addition I know of a friend's spaniel that appeared as Elizabeth Barrett Browning's dog 'Flush' in a television drama/documentary.

As much a 'hit' as *The Artist* in the media charts is the television drama *Downton Abbey*: the third series depicted a shooting scene – in which all the dogs shown were actually owned and worked by keepers and others who would normally be involved in a shooting day!

A typical picture of an Edwardian shooting scene – or is it? In actual fact the photo depicts a 'still' from the hugely successful television series *Downton Abbey*. Most important, though, is the fact that whilst 'acting' on this occasion, both handler and dogs pick up at least three times a week during the shooting season (photo courtesy of Reedlands Retrievers/Nicola Small).

Chapter 13

Coats, Clothes and Boots

A suit of clothes has always been part of the professional gamekeeper's employment package. In Victorian times, many of the village locals knew the keeper as 'Old Velveteen' – a nickname derived from the fact that his suit uniform was made up from a dark, velvet-like cloth.

As time progressed, though, the type of cloth that gave rise to the old nickname lost its popularity and many estates had suits made up of tweed cloth, the pattern of which was unique to the shoot. In many places, this practice continues today, perhaps most noticeably on the Royal estates, each of which dresses its keepers in specific tweed.

In Scotland, the stalkers, ghillies and keepers, working in a country where the best and thickest tweeds are woven, claim that their favoured material offers protection against the worst of weather, even on the hill, where there is little shelter. With that in mind, let's begin with this old shooting standby.

Talking Tweed

It's a funny material tweed: it might be waterproof, but anyone who has ever had the dubious pleasure of wearing a keeper's suit on a wet day knows that it certainly isn't lightweight and that before too many hours have passed, you will be forced to adopt a posture more akin to a gorilla than a human being in order to counteract the additional weight.

Disadvantages of tweed

In most instances, tweed is far too hot and so prickly that you cannot walk more than a few yards before the inside of your thighs feel as if they have had a close encounter with a brillo-pad wielding sadist. And it smells – it doesn't matter whether or not you send a tweed suit to the cleaners at the end of each shooting season, as soon as you open the wardrobe door in preparation for the first day of the next, the all-pervading smell will leave you wondering whether the dog took up temporary summer residence in there after a particularly good walk on the foreshore.

Cleaning tweed

In actual fact, it is not actually a very good idea for you to send a tweed suit to the cleaners; the heaviest types come back with all the individual fibres welded together, ending up with an item of clothing that more resembles a sheet of cardboard than it does something that once formed a very effective coat for sheep.

How to wear woollen stockings

What a fortune manufacturers must make on the sale of woollen stockings to accompany breeches. It is seemingly no longer acceptable to opt for a simple pair with no adornments; instead they need to be colourful and characterful, topped off with contrasting checks, embroidered game birds or, as has been seen on some shooting fields recently, swear-words.

You can even buy separate ties for the tops, but remember tradition has it that the socks must come over the buckles of the breeches and it is very bad form to adopt the sensible and logical option of keeping up one's stockings by holding them in place with the strap attachments of your breeches.

A really good country clothing and fieldsports equipment shop such as this one should be able to supply *both* traditional tweed suits and clothing made from the most modern of material. Look carefully at any labels though and make sure that whatever is chosen is likely to suit your particular purpose. Check also that, when the time comes, you can clean it (or have it cleaned) according to the manufacturer's cleaning and storing advice (courtesy of Robjent's Fine Country Pursuits Ltd).

Modern Technology

Modern technology has improved the clothing of all field sportsmen and women. The choice of waterproofs, leggings and boots is as bewildering as it is useful. Fleeces, internally leather-lined shoes, featuring self-cleaning soles which eject mud through the walking motion, Gore-Tex® and Teflon®-treated coats, and soft Loden jackets all help in keeping out the wind and rain.

Breathable fabrics are brilliant in ensuring that you get neither too hot nor cold and work by wicking away moisture. Gore-Tex® is arguably the best known of these, but there are others that do just as good a job.

Their patented manufacturing methods also help in silencing the rustle of clothing, enabling the keeper to stalk a fox or deer more efficiently and it is a pleasure to wear even a wet coat again the next day, unlike the cold, stiff, waxed Egyptian cotton that resulted in the wearer walking arms outstretched and zombie-like until such time as the material had been warmed through by body temperature.

Useful additions

Manufacturers of modern clothing have thought of your every need, whether it be a specially-designed pocket in which to keep your radio whilst in charge of the line, or easily accessible pockets for your cartridges.

A fleece will give you a little extra wind protection when worn under a jacket on cold days and most are breathable. It is also possible to buy shooting shirts designed to look good – as befitting your role as keeper – which are much warmer than the average check country-look shirt you can buy in most shops.

Best of all are the modern shooting trousers and breeches which, unlike the tweed of old, does not scratch and irritate your legs. Outwardly, the material feels soft to the touch, but despite that, the best are waterproof, windproof and breathable.

Look out for brands such as Musto, Barbour, Schöffel and Seeland; take care to read the attached labels carefully so as to reassure yourself of the following two things:

1. That you know exactly what materials the clothing is made from and whether it is likely to suit (no pun intended!) your purpose.

2. That, when the time comes, you can clean it (or have it cleaned) according to the manufacturer's cleaning and storing advice – which should be on the label.

Make sure of a good fit

Shooting clothes, especially jackets, need to fit well. It matters little what the material or how much it costs if you cannot move your arms properly because your coat or jacket is either too baggy or too tight. You'll need to be wearing it all day so it's as well to 'try before you buy' and to do so, you will obviously have to visit a shop rather than buy something online or from a glossy advert or brochure.

A warm, well-clad keeper is a happy keeper! (photo courtesy of Robert Stephenson).

Boots

Like any item of clothing, boots, especially ankle boots, take some time to wear in and feel really comfortable. Even when one has taken the precaution of 'breaking them in' by wearing them around the house and taking the dog out for exercise, it can be a totally different experience to when one is out on a big hike, the grouse moors or even, as a group of friends recently were, big game hunting in Africa where the main topic of conversation each evening appeared to have concerned who had acquired the most blisters as a result of ill-fitting footwear.

Wearing Wellingtons

There are several makers who specialise in creating quality, natural rubber boots designed expressly with the field sportsperson in mind. Long gone are the days of sloppy, ill-fitting affairs, and most by the likes of Le Chameau or Aigle incorporate a fitted design around the ankle and lower leg.

Some are leather or Gore-Tex® lined for extra warmth and comfort – and may also have the added refinement of a full-length or part-length strong YKK zip down the side, which makes both getting into and out of them a great deal easier than it is with conventional Wellingtons. You do, of course, have to pay for the privilege and such boots are not, when compared to other makes, particularly cheap.

Patching over the cracks!

Technology is constantly developing revolutionary new ideas and, from America, comes a 'peel and stick' patch designed to save fieldsports enthusiasts money by repairing rather than replacing, damaged waders, Wellingtons, kit bags and many other essential outdoor items.

Tear-Aid® is a transparent water and airtight patch for use in such situations and its manufacturers claim that it remains adhesive in both high and low temperatures, making it suitable for use in all weathers. There are two types available: an all-purpose fabric patch and a specific version for vinyl products. Each comes in a choice of patches, strips or on a roll, and can be cut with scissors for a custom-fit. For more information, visit: www.tear-aid.co.uk

---

These boots were made for walking...

Once a pair of leather boots has been properly broken in, it pays to look after them in the hope that they will give years of protection and comfort.

Always remove dirt and mud from boots and shoes, and if they are wet, stand them to dry out naturally in a warm airy place, but not right on top of a stove or radiator.

Special bags of crystals that absorb moisture can be bought to put inside boots or Wellingtons and these help to wick away the dampness from inside the boots. These bags must then be dried out before being used again. Failing that, the old traditional standby of using scrunched up newspapers stuffed inside boots certainly helps in absorbing wet resulting from walking through an over-deep puddle or stretch of water.

Cleaning leather boots

Years ago, it was accepted practice to treat outdoor boots with a good application of dubbin, allowing it to soak in and then finishing off with polish or cream. Nowadays, all my leather boots, and indeed, normal day-to-day shoes, are kept in fine form by the occasional application of the natural, but almost magical, Renapur Leather Balsam.

Even the price appeals to my tight-fisted Yorkshire nature as, despite nowadays costing around £12 for a 200g pot, it will, if my current rate of usage remains the same, easily last five years or more. It does, quite literally, what it says on the tin in that it 'protects, waterproofs and nourishes all leathers, restoring their original softness and colour, preserving its looks and so extending its life'.

There are, of course, many other products that keep boots in good repair, but remember that some are silicone-based and, whilst helping to make boots waterproof, will not necessarily 'feed' the leather in any way.

Any leather boots – be they for work-a-day use or as 'best' on a shooting day – need regular drying, cleaning and nourishing with a proprietary cleaner such as Renapur Balsam (other products are available!).

Insulated ankle boots
Launched onto the market in late 2011 was a completely new type of ankle boot (the Revel, by Keen Footwear) which, according to the manufacturer, 'delivers outstanding performance in three key challenges of winter footwear – warmth, traction and moisture management'. As regards the latter, one might assume they are talking of sweaty feet, but as regards warmth, it appears the boot has an underfoot system that functions like traditional loft insulation to trap warmth in, while keeping cold out. The insulation is formed by a three-layer 'sandwich' comprising heat-trapping honeycomb, a woollen felt layer, and a thermal heat shield designed to reflect heat back into the foot.

To keep your feet dry, the boots have a waterproof, nubuck leather upper that features a special membrane which 'offers increased breathability'.

A hybrid boot
Somewhere between a Wellington and a leather boot is the calf-length leather Wellington boot! Possibly the best known of these is the Dubarry which is made from Drifast-Drisoft leather and is Gore-Tex® lined. They, and boots of a similar

type, are getting more and more popular as each shooting season passes and those who have them, swear by them.

The country boot has a suede appearance and, as such, requires a little careful maintenance from time to time – nothing too onerous, just a careful rub with an old towel and the application of a protector spray. Other types may need special cleaners and conditioners – all of which are produced by the boot manufacturers themselves.

Don't Forget the Small Essential Items

Just as your annual holiday can be ruined by the omission of some small yet essential item, so too can a day on the shoot.

- You might think you've left your leggings in the vehicle as is your normal practice and it is no good recalling that you actually have left them hanging in the boiler room or out-house to dry after being caught in a sudden downpour the last time out.

- Items such as hats – useful to shield your face when pigeon shooting or deer stalking as well as being protection from the weather – are very easy to forget.

- Sunglasses can be very useful when out in the early autumn and the day can be marred when one realises that they have been forgotten or misplaced.

- Do you normally wear boots or Wellingtons? The former can be a lot more pleasant to wear on the dry days, but on a dewy morning, a pair of nylon 'spats' or short walking leggings will help in preventing debris from slipping down into the boots – they are also, unfortunately, very easy to forget.

- A good way of ensuring that you always keep these 'bits and pieces' with you is to allocate a canvas fishing bag purely for keeping such items together – I know of many keepers who ear-mark one purely to keep glasses, rain chokers, scarves, hats, ear defenders, dog whistles and leads all in the same place.

Ear Defenders for Loaders

Gamekeepers quite often get asked to go loading on estates where double-gunning is practised. Now in my mid-fifties, I think that it's true to say that hardly anyone of my generation ever wore hearing protection of any kind and if you did, you were looked on as being slightly odd and precious.

As I was never as interested in shooting as I was in the other aspects of gamekeeping and in the shooting day, I put the deafness in my left ear down to the fact that I'd stood for many hours loading double guns for my various employers and their friends. Science and technology thankfully make such a possibility far less likely.

Ear defenders are essential whether shooting or loading for someone else. Conventional ones work well and protect the wearer's hearing – which is, after all, the whole idea – but the most up-to-date on the market incorporate technology such as direct communication via Smart phones (photo courtesy of Elliot Hobson).

Understanding the causes

Deafness is a very serious problem amongst many shooting folk and it is not all down to the fact that we are getting older. Apparently, if you were to take the roar of a motorcycle running full-throttle for 40 hours non-stop and then condense it into a split second, you have, according to the experts, a very good approximation of the sound energy generated by an average gunshot. So, unless you have been sensible and used ear defenders throughout your shooting life, every single shot taken means that, as the years have progressed, we have all been getting slightly, but permanently, deafer.

What the scientists say

Scientists have proven that it takes very little 'sonic trauma' to cause permanent damage and that for every five years of recreational shooting a person enjoys, the risk of high-frequency hearing loss escalates by some 7 percent.

The reasons given are, apparently, all to do with the cochlea – a fluid-filled, snail shell-shaped organ buried deep in the inner ear. Sound travels through the air as pressure waves that are then directed down the ear canal to the eardrum, which vibrates. Its slight movements are relayed via three miniature bones (the hammer, stirrup and anvil) to another membrane that covers the opening of the cochlea.

When this membrane begins to dance, the vibrations are transmitted inside the cochlea's fluid-filled centre which is lined with minuscule hair-like projections called cilia that are adversely affected by high-frequency sounds. Intense noise, such as a shotgun blast, can cause vibrations so violent that they can, in effect, fell the affected cilia as an earthquake does trees.

Hear my warning!

Although impossible to totally eliminate the sound of gunshot, you can reduce them to a safer level – apparently and according to researchers, approximately 80 decibels – by the use of well designed ear defenders, or even custom-fitted earplugs. Like many others, it is perhaps too late for me to take effective preventative measures, but if you are responsible for the well-being of newcomers to shooting, never let them stand anywhere near a gun without first of all being equipped with adequate protection.

Bits and Pieces

A little like the back of the average gamekeeper's vehicle that always seems to contain a load of what, at first glance, might appear to be unnecessary equipment – but which to the keeper is absolutely vital – I include here some potentially useful information which has, however, no proper place elsewhere!

Working with the Police

Chairman of the National Gamekeepers' Organisation Lindsay Waddell is quoted as saying '...quite apart from their normal duties, it is important to realize that in many remote rural areas, gamekeepers are the eyes and ears of the law enforcement agencies'.

The NGO periodically organises courses for the benefit of police forces throughout the country in which they aim to improve law enforcement in the countryside and also to reduce the number of gamekeepers and lawful shooters wrongly arrested. Still in its early stages, the course aims to help those in authority with no background in the countryside and to help prevent misunderstandings and wrongful arrests.

Entitled 'Gamekeeping and the Law – Training for the Police', the one-day course is offered to officers and civilians who wish to learn more about what gamekeepers do and what the law actually says on things like trapping, shooting, poaching and other rural crimes.

How to remain legal yourself!

Apart from very carefully staying on the right side of the law concerning all gamekeeping matters – and ensuring that your vehicle is legal and that number-plates are always clearly visible (not always an easy matter on a muddy estate in the depths of a wet winter), there are a few other small but important points to bear in mind.

Remember to carry your shotgun certificate, especially when travelling and when there is therefore a possibility that you may be stopped as a result of a routine motorway check. In this instance, it is also as well to consider the most secure

Anyone on private ground with a dog cannot be said to be trespassing – unless that is, they are 'trespassing with intent' and using a running dog to catch hares in much the same way as a gun could be used to shoot pheasants. In places where walkers tend to stray from the path with their dogs, all one can do is to ask, either verbally or by notification, that they return to the footpath and keep their dogs on a lead. In this particular situation, the insertion of a 'please' and 'thank-you' might be less antagonistic.

method of transporting your gun so that it is not on obvious view – a factor that, quite correctly, is frowned upon by the relevant authorities. For the same reason, consider the possibility of being stopped in possession of skinning knives and the like when out on a stalking foray or similar.

Poaching

It is not a criminal offence for anyone to trespass, if that is all they are doing. If, however, you catch anyone trespassing in pursuit of game, then it is a totally different story.

Technically, one might argue that, because of the wording of the law, a pheasant, or indeed any form of game, is what is known in legal jargon as 'no property' and as such, belongs to no one when they are in the wild. Whilst this might be true, the game Acts were designed not so much to place the ownership of game into the hands of the landowner or occupier (they do not in fact do so), but to make it an offence to trespass in pursuit of them. With a gun, the offence of armed trespass would be committed.

Armed trespass

Armed trespass is not confined to anyone carrying a shotgun or rifle – for which the relevant certificates are required – but also to persons with a low-powered air rifle. It doesn't matter whether the gun is loaded or not, or even whether the person confronted has any pellets in their pockets. The mere possession of the airgun on land where the user has no permission to be is, or should be, sufficient for a conviction. Armed trespass in general is a serious criminal offence.

Car Trespass on Private Ground
Having keepered on two estates in highly populated areas of Surrey and Sussex, I know that the parking of cars can cause great problems, especially if they are left in front of gateways or down narrow tracks. If your shoot happens to suffer in this way, there are several legal options that might dissuade future parking.

• A single 'offender', a dog-walker perhaps, should be approached politely and asked to park elsewhere.

• You can apparently apply for car owner details from the Driver and Vehicle Licensing Agency (DVLA) (a small fee is charged) and then write to the owner explaining the reasons why access is required.

• If the track is privately owned, the most obvious solution is to erect a gate across the access, together with a sign saying that it is used by farm vehicles and that access for wide vehicles is required at all times.

• Consider having some large paper-based gummed stickers printed with 'You Are Parked On Private Property – Access Required 24/7' and slap one on the miscreant's windscreen; they are a nuisance to remove, but do not cause damage.

• It can be useful to erect disclaimer signs saying that the landowner cannot accept any responsibility for cars parked on private premises – they are sometimes sufficient to make people think twice about parking.

The right to roam – and other issues

No one can be convicted of simple trespass – a fact that might, on occasions, cause frustrations with casual walkers whom you find on your shoot. In some areas of the British Isles, the 'right to roam' actually puts what laws there might be on the walker's side – especially in Scotland. It is therefore pleasing to see that Scottish Natural Heritage (SNH) – who might perhaps be expected to be on the side of walkers and other casual country users – actively encourages walkers and the like to check ahead prior to going out on the hills in the hope that they won't inadvertently, or otherwise, disturb either stalking or grouse shooting in the autumn.

The SNH have developed the 'Heading for the Scottish Hills' website (www.outdooraccess-scotland.co./hftsh) which includes information about stalking seasons, contact details for shooting estates and detailed forecasts as to where and when deer culling is likely to take place.

The Rising Cost of Firearms Certificates

Costs have to go up – we all accept that. What is being currently challenged by various shooting organisations is the need for the cost of firearm and shotgun certificates to rise by a proposed 88 percent. In a paper prepared in 2012 for the Home Office by the Firearms and Explosives Licensing Working Group of the Association of Chief Police Officers (ACPO FELWG), just such proposals were made.

Who is responsible now ... and in the future?

Irrespective of what you might eventually have to pay for your firearm/shotgun certificate, one of the major bones of contention is that the reason for the increased prices is because the police authorities are claiming that 'firearms licensing is not part of core policing duties and therefore the cost of firearms licensing should not be borne by the public purse'.

The National Gamekeepers' Organisation counteracts this claim saying that the licensing of firearms has been a public duty, by law, since 1920 and that ACPO's own paper acknowledges that 'the primary objective of the firearms licensing process is to protect the public from harm'. Interestingly, in the past, whenever anyone has ever suggested that a civilian authority could be more appropriate, the police have always insisted on retaining responsibility – it will be fascinating to see what eventually happens ... and the possibility of change on such matters is something of which we should remain aware.

Extending the Shooting Season

Periodically, the question arises as to whether the current game shooting seasons are sensible. Most who think it should be changed advocate being able to shoot through into the month of February.

As the law currently stands, the pheasant season in England, Wales and Scotland lasts from 1 October until 1 February , the partridge season runs from 1 September until 1 February, and wild duck and goose seasons are from 1 September until 31 January. At the time of writing, the current Leader of the House (Parliament) has promised that he will look into the possibility of an extension to the game shooting season into February.

There are supporters both for and against. A BASC spokesman, for example, says that 'There may be strong arguments for an extension – particularly the economic benefits to the country and the growing market for game meat'. A Countryside Alliance representative thinks otherwise and comments, 'There is little desire within the shooting community to extend the season. These dates are set for practical management and conservation reasons and must be considered alongside the interests of the countryside as a whole.'

There are several patented pieces of equipment which make loading cartridges into a shotgun quicker for the single Gun – even so, there are occasions when such devices will not do and the services of the gamekeeper will be called upon to either load 'double guns' or to act as a 'stuffer'.

Double Guns and Loading

Sometimes, you as a keeper, will be asked by your employer or a regular Gun to act as a loader or 'stuffer' (the difference between the two being, of course, that a loader will be handling double guns and all that that involves, whilst a stuffer loads a single gun after it has been broken by the person shooting).

If you've never loaded before, it is important to find someone who has, and to ask them to give you a few dummy lessons. Even during a practice run, it is all too easy to clash barrels – and that is without the excitement and adrenalin rush of birds coming at you.

Practice makes perfect

Practise too a good method of keeping cartridges close to hand. Personally, I find that the best way I can be ready for a sudden flush is by holding five cartridges between my fingers, and if I can see birds coming from a long way off, will hold three more in my mouth (brass tops outwards). By doing so, it is possible for the Gun to shoot off 12 cartridges before you have to delve into pocket or cartridge bag. Other loaders have different methods, but this one works for me. By shaking the cartridge bag periodically, you will ensure that the brass tops always face upwards, making it easier to grab a handful in a hurry. Never, ever, risk taking too few cartridges to a peg – cartridges might be heavy, but having to take them back after a drive is preferable to the embarrassment of running out during it!

On the day, the loader should also establish how hard the Gun would like you to slam the guns into their hand on a changeover – it is surprising how forceful some want you to be. This gives an automatic grip reflex on the weapon that is being passed over and, bearing in mind the fact that a good shot will be looking to the horizon for on-coming birds rather than looking to see where his or her gun is being placed, helps in ensuring a safe and efficient changeover.

The loaders' responsibility

Except in wet weather, you should generally keep the gun barrels pointing upwards. The most obvious reason is for safety's sake, but from this position it is also easier to pass a loaded gun and receive the empty one quickly and efficiently.

In really bad weather conditions, it may be necessary to keep a loaded gun pointed downwards in order to prevent rainwater running down the barrels and into the action – but beware of turning and inadvertently pointing the barrels at the Gun, guest or dog.

Although there can really be no excuse for it, when handling double guns, there is a possibility that a single cartridge may be left in the breech at the end of the drive due to the changing of guns after a successful 'kill' when only one cartridge has been fired, so check, check and double-check that your guns are empty before putting them back in their sleeve.

Between drives, keep a close eye on your guns and don't leave them propped against anywhere where they may come to harm. I have seen a pair of very expensive London-made guns run over and completely written off by a Land Rover when this rule was ignored.

It is the traditional responsibility of the loader to clean the guns. Experienced loaders quite often take their own cleaning equipment to a shoot, as so many gun cases contain no cleaning gear. Gunrooms are also often ill-equipped, and the other loaders will quickly use what is available.

Once clean, make sure the guns are taken to the right vehicle, and never assume that, just because you know the Gun's car, that is where they should be placed – they could be being taken elsewhere for safe-keeping or in readiness for another shoot later in the week.

Minders and helpers

As not many estates actually shoot double guns on a regular basis, loaders and stuffers often find themselves involved more as instructors and minders for the less experienced. To do this expertly and efficiently, they do perhaps need to possess more than just a general knowledge and understanding of what is expected. It is for that reason that many who might be reasonably termed to be professional are equipped with more shooting qualifications than the average university graduate!

Suitable qualifications might include being registered as a CPSA or BASC coach/instructor, a member of the Guild of Shooting Instructors, NGO Loader certified, or holding the Lantra (loading) shooting level 2 certificates. In addition, they should also be insured.

Understanding Woodcock Migration

Woodcock are fascinating and mysterious birds and the opportunity to shoot at one as it appears from a wooded drive will engender a great deal of excitement amongst your line of Guns – so much so that they will often leave pheasants flying directly over their head in the hope of getting a chance of bringing down this most elusive bird!

Because so little is known about them, you might find yourself being asked lots of questions at the end of the drive; not the least of which might be where to locate the highly prized pin feather.

Gun and 'stuffer' in action (photo courtesy of Elliot Hobson).

When and why do woodcock arrive?

Weather conditions play a predominant role in the woodcock migration. In a generally mild winter, it is probable that any potential migrants will remain in their base areas abroad until a protracted spell of cold weather forces them to travel to the warmer regions of Great Britain. In such conditions, birds will continue to arrive long after the traditionally accepted times of late November and early December.

Many years ago, there was a common belief that woodcock only migrated on a full moon and that the majority arrived on the one that occurred nearest to Halloween, but in point of fact, it is now generally accepted that birds will migrate throughout October, November and December, depending on the weather and wind direction.

Locating that elusive pin feather!

Even if you know where on the wing they are located, they are not easy to find. All I can do is to tell you that they are on the very outside of the wing, just past the wrist joint and at the base of the leading primary. If you first pull out the primary feather, the pin feather should be visible as a small slim feather no more than 2.5cm long and about 5mm across.

What to do with it

Once found, pin feathers are traditionally inserted or super-glued to the outer band of a hat, but there is another, quite fascinating alternative which is to cut off the tip of the woodcock's top beak, in which are two tiny channels filled with a fleshy substance. The pin feathers are then gently pushed into this and the tip of the mandible left to dry naturally. The 'flesh' apparently hardens and holds the feathers securely in the little natural mount which can then be attached to your hat or, if you are particularly skilled at such things, perhaps even made into a brooch.

I see from a trawl of the internet that it is possible to purchase commercially made sterling silver woodcock-shaped 'brooches' into which your pin feathers can be inserted.

Walking Sticks

Efficient keepers will ensure that there is a plentiful supply of beating sticks cut and ready for the beginning of the season. By Christmas, however, their stocks will no doubt have diminished due to the fact that certain members of the beating team have 'adopted' them as their own! Whether you are a keeper, beater, picker-up or Gun, there is something quite comforting about having a selection of sticks kept ready and waiting in the hallstand or utility room.

I know several people who have a stick for all occasions: perhaps a horn-handled job for walking the dog, a tall, forked one to act as a rifle rest, a shooting stick for the infrequent days when one is asked as a guest to a driven shoot and a selection suitable for bashing about in the brambles.

Beating sticks

A good beating stick soon becomes a vital part of your equipment and the day can be spoilt if it is forgotten and one has to borrow an inferior one from the beater's shed. Almost any wood will do, but most appear to be cut from hazel, no doubt because hazel is the straightest and easiest to come across.

Undoubtedly holly makes the best beating stick and lasts longest. If you take the time to look at the base of a little clump of hollies and scrape about at the base, you can often find a section growing from another that will form a very comfortable and natural handle, or even a small lump of root which, once dried and shaped, will fit very comfortably in the cupped hand. I've had several over the years, all of which have become favourites due to their individual characteristics; however, as is the way of all things, they eventually get broken or lost.

Whistles

A whistle of one kind or another is invaluable to the gamekeeper, either when hand-feeding your pheasants on a daily basis or to signal the start and finish of a drive on a shooting day.

Woodcock are possibly the most interesting and prettiest of any sporting quarry; equally as interesting and pretty is this carved walking stick depicting the heads of two such birds in amazingly accurate detail. To create as an immaculate a masterpiece takes a great many man-hours and it would be pure folly to take a stick of this standard out beating! (photo courtesy of Robert Stephenson).

Using a whistle hand-feeding

I always believed in hand-feeding my birds and, in order to attract them to the feed ride, would always whistle by mouth. Fortunately, my natural whistle is so loud that it could be heard from far away – in fact, one or two of the estate's households used my regular morning signal as an alarm call! For those not blessed with such strong lungs, a football whistle or similar will work just as well; the only disadvantage being that you may forget an artificial whistle, whereas it's impossible to forget your mouth. A cold, frosty morning can, however, prevent your mouth from being able to whistle, but I've always found that a little saliva and a vigorous rubbing of the lips with the tip of your forefinger will remedy the situation.

Indicating the start and finish of a drive

You cannot beat a whistle for indicating the finish of a drive. The cheap and tacky horns used by many keepers for the same purpose sound more like a bull calf stuck in a ditch rather than a clear-cut signal that shooting is over and it is time to put

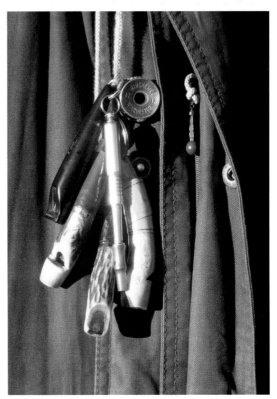

Whistles of varying types are a handy tool for the keeper: they can be used to attract pheasants when hand-feeding, as an indicator of the beginning or end of a drive and, perhaps most obviously, as a means of signalling working gundogs.

guns away in their slips. A clear and strident blast from a good quality whistle, on the other hand, leaves no one in any doubt whatsoever.

There is also the added advantage that a whistle can be attached by a lanyard and either hung around the neck or slipped into the top jacket pocket of a keeper's suit; while, it seems, from what I've observed, most keepers who use the dreaded horns, tend to stuff them in their pocket – from where it is easy to lose them whilst scrabbling about under brambles and over ditches.

An End of Season 'Tidy-Up'

No matter how tidy you are throughout the season, there's always a little bit of tidying up to do once all the Guns have gone home and it's time to start thinking about the next season. Here's a short check-list of things that are so easy to overlook:

• Any small bales of straw left intact as 'look-out points' on the feed rides should have their strings cut and the contents spread: the operation is not as simple as you would imagine and what were sweet-smelling easily handled golden bales in September will be black, soggy and totally unmanageable by now. A pitchfork is the easiest answer. (If the ride is situated in a game crop, it is not enough to merely cut the strings in the hope that the tractor and plough will spread them for you when it comes to preparing the ground in April: from experience all that happens is the bales get caught in the plough shares and get you into the bad books of the tractor driver.)

• Remember that feed bag which blew out of the back of your vehicle just before Christmas? Yes, that's right, the one you threaten to pick up from the ditch every time you drive past but never do! Pick it up now, especially if yours is a rented shoot and the contract is coming up for renewal – landlords do not generally look favourably on rubbish lying around their ground.

• Electric fencing units used around the release pens should come in now. Remember to remove the batteries if you don't want to find a leaking congealed mess when you next need them. As you put them away, smear a good covering of Vaseline or similar protective jelly over the terminals and if any are suspected of being faulty, take them into your local agricultural supplier for a service and overhaul – it will cost money, but not as much as if you forget and a fox finds his way into a pen of newly released poults next summer.

• Had you followed the suggested advice in the 'Code of Good Shooting' issued by the BASC, any sections used as partridge release pens would have been removed and stored a few weeks before the first shooting day, but if for some reason you neglected to do this, it's time to get them in the dry in order to give them a fresh coating of wood preservative and replace any loose nails or wire netting staples.

Glossary

Addled: A fertile egg, the embryo of which has died during incubation.

Air sac: Air space found at the broad end of the egg.

Ancient woodland: Any woodland which has existed from pre-1600 to the present day.

ASNW: Ancient Semi-Natural Woodland.

ATV: All Terrain Vehicle.

Baffle-boards: Boards around the bottom of rearing pen sections which act as a wind-break.

Bag: Total number of birds or animals shot in a day.

Beat keeper: Keeper who works under a headkeeper but is responsible for his own part of the estate.

Beater: Person who flushes game for shooting.

Beetle banks: Two-metre grass strips through the middle of arable fields. Such fields can be managed as one unit, as the headland is still cropped.

Bitting: The action of fitting anti-peck bits between the upper and lower mandibles of a poult.

BOAT: Byway Open to All Traffic.

Brood spot: Bare patch found on the breast of a broody hen.

Broody hens: Chickens or bantams used for sitting and hatching a clutch of eggs.

Butts: The name given to hides in which Guns stand on the grouse moors (or around a flight pond).

Caeca: The last part of a game bird's gut.

Candling: Using a strong source of light to reveal the contents of a whole egg and judge its fertility.

Close season: Dates during which a quarry species is protected by law and may not be killed.

Codes of practice: Sets of rules by which the shooting/gamekeeping/rearing fraternity self-regulates its behaviour.

Coppice: Small wood consisting of underwood and small trees grown for the purpose of periodic cutting; expanse of deciduous shrubs or trees which are cut back to near ground level at regular intervals to provide a crop of useable and sustainable timber.

Corvid: Group of bird types, members of which include magpies, jays, rooks and crows.

Crop: Place in which food is stored after swallowing, but before it travels through to the bird's stomach and gizzard.

CROW: As well as being a bird that takes game bird eggs, CROW is an acronym for Countryside and Rights of Way Act 2000 which includes the 'right to roam'.

Cull: To kill selectively (especially old or weak) individuals.

Decoy: A dummy (or, in the case of a Larsen trap, live bird) used to lure other birds.

DEFRA: Department of Environment, Food and Rural Affairs.

Dogging-in: Flushing game back in to the centre of the shoot from the boundaries to prevent them from wandering.

Double-gunning: When a Gun uses two shotguns and the services of a loader.

Driven game: Form of sport in which birds are flushed over a team of standing Guns.

Duodenum: The first part of the game bird's small intestine. It receives digestive enzymes and bicarbonate from the pancreas and bile from the liver. Digestion is completed here before the food moves to the lower small intestine for nutrient absorption.

Egg tooth: Small 'spike' at the tip of the upper beak; it enables the game bird chick to chip its way out of the egg and disappears several hours after hatching.

Electric energiser: Unit used to supply power to electric fencing.

Flight feathers: The large primary feathers in the last half of the wing.

Flight pond: Area of water into which wildfowl drop to feed and/or rest.

Flush: To put up game.

Ghillie: A guide, particularly in Scotland, who accompanies shooters or fishermen.

Gibbet: At one time it was the practice of many keepers to hang dead predators and vermin on a washing line affair, or nail them to the back of a shed so that their employers could see that they had been doing their job.

Thankfully, a 'gamekeeper's gibbet' is never nowadays seen.

Gizzard: Grinding stomach of game bird with muscular lining for pulping food.

Head keeper: Person in overall charge of running the shoot and who has one or more keepers working with him.

Head (of game): Number shot.

Infra-red: Type of heating used for rearing chicks.

Jugging: Partridges do not roost and instead squat overnight in coveys on the ground, a practice known as 'jugging'.

Keel-bone: An alternative name for a bird's breast-bone.

Keyes® trays: Flat fibre trays used for egg storing.

Lamping: Night shooting of pests and predators using a powerful spotlamp.

Larsen traps: Legal and effective 'cage' traps used to control members of the crow family.

Mandible: Lower or upper half of beak.

Manor: An old-fashioned term used to describe a partridge shooting estate.

Monoflex: Heavy plastic material reinforced with mesh squares for added strength; often used as a covering for night shelters on the rearing field.

Moulting: The period when a bird sheds its old feathers and re-grows new ones.

Open season: Dates during which quarry species may be taken legally, also known as the shooting season.

Pegging: 'Pegging out' is not what keepers do when exhausted at the end of the day – more the action of positioning and placing pegs to indicate where Guns should stand on each drive. Alternatively, 'pegging' can mean when a dog either in the beating line or picking-up captures and retrieves an unshot bird.

Pegs: Markers placed at intervals at the end of a wood or cover crop at which Guns stand to shoot.

Picker-up: Person who retrieves dead and wounded game with the aid of gundogs.

Predator: Animals or birds which hunt for food.

Proventriculus: Also known as the 'true stomach' – the part of the bird's stomach where digestion begins.

PROW: Public Rights of Way – a general term for both public footpaths and public bridleways.

Public bridleway: A route along which the general public have a legal right of passage on (or leading) a horse, on (or pushing) a pedal cycle or on foot.

Public footpath: A route along which the general public have a right of passage on foot only.

Release pens: Sectioned areas of woodland into which young pheasant poults are placed in order to acclimatise to natural conditions after being kept on the rearing field.

Rough shooting: See 'Walked-up'.

Running dogs: Coursing dogs, generally used by poachers.

Scatter feeding: Spreading grain on a feed ride so that pheasants have something to interest them and keep them busy and occupied.

Secondary feathers: Quill feathers on the wing, which are usually visible when the wings are either folded or extended.

Sewelling: Long strips of thin plastic tied to a length of cord and used to encourage birds to fly from a flushing point.

'Straights': An expression used by the feed industry to describe non-medicated supplementary feed such as cereal.

Sustainable harvest: The amount which can be shot without detriment to the population as a whole.

Syndicate: Group of people who shoot together, sharing the costs of a day's or season's sport.

Trachea: Otherwise known as the windpipe and is part of the respiratory system that allows air to pass from the larynx to the lungs and bronchi. Sometimes the trachea can be affected by dust and worm infections.

Treading: Action of male bird mating with female.

'Trickle-release': An expression mainly used when releasing partridges whereby a few are carefully liberated from the holding pen over a period of time.

Under-keeper: Keeper, usually young or a trainee, who reports directly to the headkeeper and generally assists rather than having his own 'beat'.

Understory: Generally accepted to mean the lower canopies of hazel and similar growing under mature trees such as oak.

Vermin: See 'Predator'.

Walked-up: Form of shooting in which the shooter flushes the quarry as he walks through cover.

Wildfowler: Person who shoots ducks and geese on the foreshore.

Index